Changing the World Through Children

Ruth Dutting Witte

BALBOA PRESS

A DIVISION OF HAY HOUSE

Balboa Press books may be ordered through booksellers or by contacting:

Balboa Press
A Division of Hay House
1663 Liberty Drive
Bloomington, IN 47403
www.balboapress.com
1 (877) 407-4847

Because of the dynamic nature of the Internet, any web addresses or links contained in this book may have changed since publication and may no longer be valid. The views expressed in this work are solely those of the author and do not necessarily reflect the views of the publisher, and the publisher hereby disclaims any responsibility for them.

The author of this book does not dispense medical advice or prescribe the use of any technique as a form of treatment for physical, emotional, or medical problems without the advice of a physician, either directly or indirectly. The intent of the author is only to offer information of a general nature to help you in your quest for emotional and spiritual well-being. In the event you use any of the information in this book for yourself, which is your constitutional right, the author and the publisher assume no responsibility for your actions.

Any people depicted in stock imagery provided by Getty Images are models,
and such images are being used for illustrative purposes only.
Certain stock imagery © Getty Images.

Art and Illustrations Credit:
Cover art - Asichka
Kids in Tree - JoAnne Moore
Family in Garden - JoAnne Moore
Seedling - JoAnne Moore
Parent Center Logo - JuliAnn Severson
Metamorphosis - Samantha Gibson

ISBN: 978-1-9822-3532-1 (sc)
ISBN: 978-1-9822-3533-8 (e)

Print information available on the last page.

Balboa Press rev. date: 10/17/2019

CONTENTS

CHAPTER

ONE

Life History of a Child Garden

Growing Places is a grassroots organization involving the tending of children. It is a life long dream which germinated while I was in college over 40 years ago- a child garden, if you will. What started as a clear vision morphed into something we could not have imagined, involving not only young children, but the broader community, and world as well.

I created *Growing Places (GP)* as an enrichment program for young children, in the basement of my home 25 years ago. What started as a summer program in the areas of nature and creativity was incorporated into curriculum for preschoolers, and for after school enrichment.

As the years passed, *The Parent Center* and *Tree Top Haven Women's Retreat* were created as resources and supportive gathering places for parents seeking social opportunity and friendship for themselves and their children.

Through a bequest from my parents, Richard and Carol Dutting, the generosity of my husband, Tony Witte, and an abundance of community support and expertise, I have been allowed the astonishing gift of realizing a program that addresses what children in today's society truly need in order to thrive and to make the world a better place.

In 2001, I purchased property in the village of Dansville, New York and established a non-profit corporation. An Advisory Board consisting of teachers, parents, business people, professionals, and community members was formed. Bylaws were developed; 501c3 federal tax exemption established.

With visions of a magical secret garden space for young children, we cleared a bit of the gravel that blanketed the play space, filled the hole with fertile soil and planted a young weeping cherry tree. I imagined the sapling, and the garden that ensued, to be symbolic of the realization of my vision. Given a suitable environment, blossoming children thrive and flourish, both individually and within their community.

The garden is a grand metaphor for life, whether it thrives and flourishes, or becomes over run and choked out by weeds. Throughout the growth and development of *Growing Places*, this metaphor has been infinitely useful in creating a vision, making preparations, and understanding why certain things haven't worked.

A life dream is as unique as any garden, neither of which is ready made, nor accurately foreseen. They must each be cultivated, and nurtured with love and patience. Conditions need to be right for either to come into bloom or fruition, in the way that encouragement of a child's creativity and problem solving skills is necessary.

Consider the rocky foundation initially provided as the palette for this lovely parcel (life, dream). A thick layer of gravel for use as planting medium is not conducive to the soul nurturing paradise I have envisioned. The speed with which the water (or funding, expertise, and moral support) runs through gravel doesn't allow the root systems to absorb the hydration necessary for growth; the plants wither and die. Certainly, children require good role models, emotional support, and acceptance to become rooted in life.

One of the first steps in moving forward with any undertaking is to get ready, lay the groundwork, develop a strong network of roots (family, friends, mentors). Before planting, it is necessary to prepare the earth- make a plan, remove the obstacles, and provide soil rich with nutrients (resources, expertise, community support). The instability of a project not well thought out crumbles and does not allow the roots to take hold and nurture the plants (children, enterprise, creative endeavor). Children need consistency, and to know what to expect. There must be commitment on behalf of parents and teachers to work together, and to follow through in showing kids how to successfully navigate the ups and downs in life.

Gardens need pollination by the wind, and by insects and birds (ideas and people from different backgrounds) if they are to grow. The level of involvement and turnover of our support system will vary, depending on the duties and willingness to carry them out. Some of our people provide the expertise required to reach a specific short term goal (acquiring tax-exempt status, or creating a successful and on-going fundraiser) before moving on after a year or two, much as an annual or biennial is used to fulfill a current desired effect. Other people commit for a longer stretch, seeing that yearly traditions (annual celebrations, or a particular service project) are well established in the way that perennials serve to create a framework for the garden. Each *GP* attendant (community member, volunteer, teacher, and family) has a specific, critical part to play in the overall metamorphosis and splendor of the garden.

Gardens (and dreams) need to be protected from from infection or attack. We need to be vigilant against burn-out, negativity, fear, and unnecessary clutter that act as weeds-pests that interfere with optimal growth of the garden.

The thick gnarly root of an unwanted vine is not unlike being so set in our ways as to become immovable and impervious to change. For instance, bittersweet is a beautiful, but tenacious creeper vine; it proceeds to choke a rose bush in much the same way that stubborn resistance to change impedes our capacity for personal development; it is bound and determined to override the desire for new growth. Negotiation, compromise, and realistic expectations are what is needed to keep the vision alive.

Gardens need cutting back. One loses sight of the beauty of the coveted blossom through trivialities and distractions. You buy a flower (turn on the television, pick up an electronic device; open a bottle of wine perhaps) that you are convinced will improve the quality of your garden. This pretty thing goes about the daily business of growing, invading the root space of other beauties (reading, playing out doors, interacting with others). You don't want to get rid of it entirely, but as long as it has space in the plot of life it becomes greedy, taking over more than was originally intended. Too much of a good thing turns out to be detrimental, just as sweltering sun leads to dehydration and burn out, withering the soul of the individual.

Aphids (inadequacy, depression, lack of boundaries and self-discipline) drain a plant of its life-giving force only until they are enjoyed by a hungry ladybug (one who has the expertise, inspiration, self-confidence and wherewithal to accomplish a task). Worms aerate the soil, offering themselves up to a bright eyed robin seeking energy for the task of creating a cozy haven for its nestlings, which in turn feast upon a veritable banquet of garden pests. A spider weaves its trap for the voracious mosquitoes that love to engorge themselves upon the gardener.

The young weeping cherry central to my child garden becomes injured, a festering wound (poor economy, marital discord) threatening its very life. Yet with patience and faith that whatever happens will provide further opportunity, it survives these growing pains, becoming all the stronger as a result.

The transformation of the children's garden space over the years has been breathtaking. It has flourished, creating a haven not only for the local wildlife, children and families, but offering a place of solace to all who enter. The laughter and the audible sighs of contentment are the gentle breezes, the wind song of life.

Through the years:

- Well over 300 children have passed through our Playschool, a preschool alternative *Growing Places* offered from 1995-2017. People traveled from a radius of up to 30 miles to attend this unique program.
- Innumerable school-aged children (including many *GP* alumni) have attended summer programs, and special events through the years, as well as intermittent after-school programs, and opportunities for home-schooled children.[i]
- Parents have been offered a common sense approach to parenting that enhances good communication, teaches respect, self-discipline, environmental awareness, and more through parent support groups, newsletters, and a newspaper column. [1]
- The children's garden expanded from a barren graveled and fenced in area, to a beautiful play space, complete with small pond dug by the children and a memorial brick path. This ever evolving wildlife habitat developed by the *Growing Places* community over the years, has provided a backdrop to nature study and environmental awareness.
- Meaningful participation in numerous community and world service organizations (Sr. Nutrition Center, Food Pantry, American Friends Service Committee, UNICEF, Heifer Project, Christian Children's Fund, and ChildFund International), have helped to build a strong foundation for social responsibility.
- For five years *Growing Places* joined forces with an indigent preschool in Dominica, West Indies. Children exchanged letters and artwork; and *Growing Places* initiated a lunch program for malnourished children.
- Opportunities for community service and internships have been made available to middle and high school students, as well as students from nearby colleges.
- A book of *Growing Places Kid's* observations and insights has been published and offered as incentive for donation.
- We launched a 20 year commemorative website detailing the *Growing Places* experience and community, as well as providing a parenting resource.[2]

---

[1] *See http://goldenratiodesign.com/growingplaces/parent-center/#changingtheworldthroughchildren*
[2] *See http://goldenratiodesign.com/growingplaces*

- Most worthy of mention is the fact that all of this to date, has been accomplished almost exclusively through volunteer service by parents and community members.

Growing Places has always made optimal use of our community's human resources. Parent, family, and community involvement have been pivotal to its development, as well as to our children's well-being and spirit of cooperation.

The power of a good pool of volunteers is staggering, for there are so many necessary chores that are simply taken for granted by the casual observer. Volunteerism serves to create a healthier society as participants realize our interdependence through service to one another.

Through the years *GP* participants (board members, parents, families) have been encouraged to make the program what they need it to be. It has provided a platform for self expression and fulfilled a desire to do something significant in the lives of so many. Volunteers have contributed to *GP*'s heritage by taking the initiative on numerous projects that had not been part of the original vision. It has evolved into what members of the *Growing Places* community have created.

- Two young mothers longing for comradery with others and social opportunity for their little ones, established a playgroup for toddlers. It has remained a staple through the years, and provided a gateway for extended involvement in the *GP* community.
- Three stay at home moms who signed their children up 15 years ago, never left.
  - One, a former Peace Corp volunteer started attending the play group with her girls. By the time they had each completed the two year Playschool program several years later, she had introduced the multicultural component so central to our philosophy. She went on to initiate a group for home-schooling families, using the space and resources at her disposal through *Growing Places*.
  - Another started our annual community-wide pumpkin contest and fundraiser in 2006. Over the years, the field of contestants has grown to involve National Honor Society students in the middle and high schools, high school art students, scouts, church groups, and other people in the community. Perhaps most significantly, it has allowed the *GP* tribe to create the family tradition of joining former classmates in our annual pumpkin carving and pizza party.
  - The third Mom was a caterer in a former life. Her brainchild was *A Taste of Dominica*, a fundraiser dinner we held for several years to educate the community about our work with a preschool in that tiny country. As a result, we initiated a lunch program for the malnourished children of our sister school in Dominica.
- The retired principal of our elementary school managed to get several years in receipts documented, and then had the gumption to establish our tax-exempt status.

- Our home school resource person went on to became the health and wellness educator at the local hospital, and our liaison for wellness related grant applications and hospital tours.
- The engineer who came to design our memorial brick path, was longing for access to a center for women. With her help and that of a medical transcriptionist who was seeking "something more" for herself at the time, *Tree Top Haven* came to life. It has offered a sense of community among women, and opportunities for personal discovery and growth in a nurturing environment.
- The retired art teacher from our middle school joined *GP* through *Tree Top Haven* to share her talents with "wannabe" artists that had their creativity squashed before they were 10; she also stepped in for a year when I needed an assistant in the classroom.

In the blink of an eye, we were creating volunteer opportunities for former students who had been inducted into the National Honor Society. One spring a crew of them came and gave *GP* the face lift it so desperately needed- painting the building exterior, creating a breath-taking mural, expanding the garden. Nostalgia and gratitude for their years at *Growing Places* and the friendships they had shared through the years as a result, were an added bonus.

A beloved music teacher in the public school system had become involved as a third grader the year *GP* was established, and went on to assist me for the next *eight* summers. I was not able to run the program the summer she graduated from high school. As she so convincingly pointed out, she had the experience and wherewithal to run it for me; and so she did. What an accomplishment for one who has not yet attended college! [3]

Many *Growing Places Kids* have returned year after year to participate in our activities and assist in various projects, before moving on to their greater purpose in life. Personal involvement with *Growing Places* has created a community-based pride in being an active participant of, and contributor to something so meaningful.

Contact with many of *GP*'s alumni, has revealed that most have been high achievers in school and extracurricular activities, going on to become very accomplished in their endeavors. I have been astonished by the successes of the *Growing Places Kids* I have followed through the years. By way of local papers and social media, I have kept up with their activities and accomplishments: citizens of the month, consistent honors achievements; participation in various community service activities; excellence in the arts and/or sports. Many have gone on to become fine artists, gifted musicians, educators, engineers, doctors, writers, and renowned athletes. What a joy it has been to bear witness

---

[3] *There is so much more to be said about many others who have brought a great deal to this organization. Scrolling through the* It Takes a Village *portion of our website is like watching the end credits of a movie, and provides more information about many others who have left their mark on Growing Places. See* <u>*http://goldenratiodesign.com/ growingplaces/it-takes-a-village/*</u>

as they blossom and thrive through the years; and to so clearly recall in my mind and heart, the little people they had been.

Because of the way *Growing Places* has operated (small groups of 6-7 children, limited hours), we could not be pigeon-holed under the state auspices of daycare or education. While the issues of safety have been strictly adhered to, we have not been bound to state regulation regarding curriculum and testing. Many of the state mandates, to our way of thinking, interfere with allowing the natural development and proper socialization needs of young children. This has given us a lot of leeway to create the kind of program that has made *Growing Places* unique.

If we'd had a "how to manual" when we started, we could have achieved in five years what took 20 years to accomplish. This book is a step by step guide incorporating best practices; a recipe for developing a program that has succeeded in shifting a tiny piece of our world into a less competitive, more accepting and nurturing environment; where each person is able to meet their best potential and has a stake in helping others to do the same.

C H A P T E R

TWO

A Necessary Alternative

The early childhood program, which has become the core of *Growing Places*, was intended as a temporary stop gap to pay the bills when I was operating out of my home; not at all part of the original plan. As the "preschool" portion of the program started to define *Growing Places* on a community level, Universal Pre-Kindergarten (UPK) was introduced into the public school system. While the other private preschools in our village were forced to close, *Growing Places* offered a unique alternative.

Here's the thing. Where UPK begins to address academics at such a young age, there is a palpable neglect in teaching self-awareness and behaviors that are conducive to a broader harmony in society at large.

Growing Places starts with nurturing and guiding a child's spirit. The expansive perception and wisdom that is so instinctive in little children becomes encroached upon through time, by the expectations and judgments of those who enter into a child's world. We strive to develop the means to accept and protect the wonder of individuality in themselves and others. Through the years we have tweaked and brought our best practices forward to make *GP* what it has become.

An unfortunate by-product of Education today has inadvertently become not to enrich curiosity and love of learning, but to instill worry about how we measure up to what someone else is doing, and fear of failure. In our society, success is all about being the smartest, fastest, most knowledgeable, very best at something- the more and faster, the bigger the better.

Progress and advancement can be good; but too much focus on advancing rapidly at a young age usually leads to the neglect of some of the most critical elements in a strong foundation for fulfillment in today's society.

There is so much pressure on children, and us as parents, to live up to the standards of the people around us. Over the years I have watched as more and more is expected of little ones. Where Kindergarten was once a time for play and first grade for learning to read and add, these are more commonly expected of children as young as 3 and 4 years old. There is a compulsion to teach kids more, better, faster, younger so they will have the "highest advantage" in life. I want to laugh and cry when I see educational materials designed to create little geniuses; and when the children can't live up to being the best, most brilliant, most athletic, most fashionable kid on the block, excelling at each thing put before them, then clearly they (or their parents) are a failure; if only in their own minds.

Little children have a great deal of critical nurturing that is being overlooked entirely as a result of the current lifestyle in our society. Many more children are attending daycare while both parents must work to make a living. Blended families require children to reconcile two living situations, often with different expectations. The sense of safety in this world has become diminished to the point of not only raising the anxiety of parents, but limiting the freedom of children to explore as we were able to growing up. Electronic devices have largely replaced the ability to find spiritual satisfaction within oneself, with a desperate search for external gratification from a young age. Little time is set aside for strengthening a sense of individuality and acceptance of self and others.

In the scurry of day to day living, we tend to forget that it takes significant time and patience to teach children to understand and cope with the myriad of feelings that wash through us every day; to learn how to communicate effectively with others, and to understand that we each, no matter who we are, have something worthwhile to offer this world.

The glorious seedling that is a child's spirit needs to be protected, and nurtured, and strengthened. Mitigating circumstances can choke this wondrous predisposition through lack of self-confidence, sense of powerlessness, isolation, and continual comparison of oneself to others.

Young children need to learn about who they are, what they are capable of, and how to express themselves in a peaceful manner. They need to learn to accept themselves and others for who they are, and about treating others with dignity and respect. The current focus of early education leaves little opportunity to address these things sufficiently.

I have come to believe that the thing that matters most is that children are fully aware of their own inner light, that they are able to call on their inner resources: creativity, courage, contentedness, acceptance, forgiveness, and happiness. We need to teach children at a young age to keep an open mind and heart; to maintain an awareness of their world and their impact on the people around them; to look at their influence in the grand scheme of things.[ii] In order to help kids achieve this, parents need grounding, community support, and resources in raising children with today's rapidly changing and often bewildering expectations.

If there is to be a more hopeful tomorrow, there needs to be a strong attitudinal shift in the way we bring children up. And if that is to happen, we need to reignite that flame within ourselves as well. We need to mulch and protect life's garden, and rediscover the beauty within ourselves and each other. This is a mighty task, but it can be done.

CHAPTER

THREE

Planting the Seeds

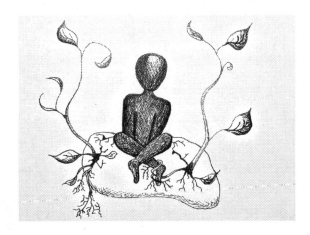

Our Days

One walks into the building to see children's artwork and lovely murals on the walls. Beautiful, soothing music (world, classical, new age) drifts through, and a feeling of joy and comfort settles in. The roomy environment is designed to give children opportunities to be involved in a variety of ways, offering specific areas for intellectual activities (puzzles, games, exploration); creative development (art); active play (balls and hula hoops, musical activity); make-believe (costumes and props); and relaxation with the quiet comfort of books and casual conversation. The garden offers a place of solace. Nooks and crannies provided by sunflowers, a weeping cherry, a goldfish pond, and playhouse are the back drop for elaborate make believe, space to run around, hideaways for quiet chats, or just a peaceful moment to oneself.

Units and broad themes are seasonal and based on children's interests. There may be an initial plan for the day, but if the children become involved with a particular project of their own choosing, the focal point for the day may change dramatically. While sequenced activities are scheduled so the children know what to expect, flexibility is critical as needs and interests of the children are identified. A large block of time may be required to complete a certain activity, or it may definitely not be a good time for a story![4] Story, play, and snack time are the constants in our day, around which music, art, field trips, and other activities revolve. [iii]

Time	A Day: Art & Social Studies	B Day: Math & Science
9-9:10	Garden Walk	Garden Walk
9:10-9:30	Musical Run Around * Parade * Dance * Lets Pretend * Songs	Physical Run Around * Slide * Tunnel * Scooters * Hopping Sacks * Balls * Hula Hoops
9:30-9:45	Welcome Circle	Welcome Circle
10-10:45	Play & Project	Play & Project
10:45-11:15	Runaround & Snack	Runaround & Snack
11:15-11:30	Play & Project	Play & Project
11:30-12	Closing Circle	Closing Circle
Social Studies one day, and Sciences the next.	Self Family Friends Community World Peace	Senses Weather Seasons Hibernation/Migration Health & Safety Life Cycle Garden/Back Yard

- **A daily walk around the garden** allows the children to observe the day-to-day changes in season and life cycle. We do this as caregivers are signing their children in. Children are asked to dress for weather.
- **Runaround time** provides physical activity necessary to build flexibility, cardiovascular fitness, and muscle strength. It is a chance for the children to get exercise as they expend pent up energies allowing for focus on the lessons for the day. During the nicer weather, much of our time is spent in the garden.

---

[4] *There are certain things that work really well in changing the level and type of energy in the classroom. Getting everyone to take three deep breaths rarely fails. Calming music helps keep the level of craziness down. We used to have an aquarium that served as time out. Putting the kids (and/or myself!) in front of the fish tank has worked like magic in calming all of us down; and you can have great conversations while watching the fish!*

- **Welcome Circle** allows for our group to come together, and to discuss the plan and behavioral expectations for the day. Our days are much calmer as a result of discussing how we will co-exist during our time together, *before* we get started.

We will be respectful.
- *We will be polite and use good manners.*
- *We will share and take turns. If you bring a toy that you don't feel like sharing, it can stay in your cubby or backpack.*
- *We will not invade personal space.*
- *We will give each other privacy when needed.*
- *We will not disrupt someone else's work (knock over towers, draw on someone's artwork).*

We will help each other as needed.
- *If one of our friends needs help (eg, in the bathroom), the teacher will help that child while the others continue to play quietly.*
- *Everyone helps everyone to pick up and put things where they belong.*
- *Tattling is not okay, unless someone is hurt or in danger. It is okay to ask for help if you have tried but can't work something out yourselves.*

The children also have the (limited) undivided attention of the rest of the group as they each take a turn speaking about things that are important to them.
- **Play and Project** time permits the teacher to work individually with each child while the other children play and learn to work things out together.
- **Runaround and Snack** allows kids to let off steam as they wait for their turn to wash hands for snack.
- **Closing Circle** allows for discussion of difficulties encountered during the day, and problem solving. Brain teasers,[5] songs, and stories are relative to the topic for the day, or just for the heck of it.

---

[5] *Brain teasers are an extensive list of questions for use during snack time and transition to circle time. These inquiries involve basic concepts (shapes, colors), self (senses, body parts, feelings), relationships in time and space, word games (rhyming, opposites, synonyms), occupations, and use of common objects. They are mixed up, so the children are flexing their minds in various ways to figure out the answers (memory, common sense, imagination). It lets us know the extent of a child's understanding, and gives us insight into their thought processes and the brilliance of their perceptions of the world. Asking children lots of questions is great for language development and improves communication skills; a child needs to collect his/ her thoughts in order to come up with an answer that makes sense. This is a learned skill, and initially a child may not know how to appropriately respond when asked a question. It's also likely to put a child on the spot. If they don't know, or don't want to speak an answer, they may "pass." As they watch others participate, before they are even aware of it, they can't hold themselves back any longer. (The same is true for participating in a game or activity) The children learn self-restraint as they withhold answers until it is their turn, and discover that they are more knowledgeable than they realized. Because they are desensitized in this manner, they are largely spared the terror of being called upon in class in the coming years.*

An Alternative Approach to Literacy

A basic credo of *Growing Places* is that there are many things a child needs to do and learn before s/he/"they"[6] are ready to read and write; and that it is not necessary or even desirable for children of preschool age to be able to identify and write their letters (unless they are chomping at the bit to do so). Attempting to force the issue of reading and writing prematurely not only detracts from other lessons of early childhood, it can cause frustration, a feeling of inferiority, and even a life long resistance to reading.

It is, however, so important to lay the groundwork which will make the task of learning to read and write easier when the time does come. We do this on a daily basis through our play, circle time, art, music activities, and lots of books, each of which play a significant role in this process.

Our day usually orbits around the books we read during circle time. Books are carefully selected for content, beauty of illustration, and quality of writing. It is clear that the earlier a love of books is instilled, the greater a passion for reading and learning as children grow.

The first couple of days with a new group of children are spent making a portfolio sized envelope with their name done in mosaic form (bits of cut paper or crumpled tissue paper). Each child chooses a section of the classroom wall on which to display their artwork through the year. This not only serves to identify a child's art space; the kids learn to recognize each other's names. Children accomplish this at different rates, and it does not take long to figure out who is proficient enough to help the others find their name in other places (coat hook, cubbyhole) until they are able to recognize it themselves. Furthermore, the envelope stores artwork as the seasons change, creating beautiful collections that can be shared at the end of the year in various community spaces.

A significant part of our program involves interviewing each child regarding our current unit of study, a recent field trip, or other important topics in life (friendship, peace, family, gratitude). Their responses to these inquiries are recorded on paper and read back to them upon completion. In doing this, communication skills are enhanced through thoughtful examination of feelings, experiences, and the world in which we live. Observing each word being written as it is dictated allows children to make the connection between written and spoken word. In the process, they learn to communicate in a coherent manner about things that are important to them. Dictations[iv] are then shared with the group. Each child listens for "their words" and also tries to guess who else has said what, paying close attention as they do so. In this way, they become mentors for one another, as kids discover new things and different perspectives from each other. At the end of the year, pages are compiled into *Me and My World*, a lovely snapshot of each child in their fourth or fifth year of life.[7]

---

[6] *"They" has come to be used in the singular, as a preferred pronoun for those who do not identify as male or female, or identify as non-binary*

[7] *See http://goldenratiodesign.com/growingplaces/wp-content/uploads/2014/08/Me-and-My-World-2012.pdf*

Further, the children become involved in making topical books. A broad selection of photos is offered for inclusion, illustrating different concepts and situations in lieu of actual experience (for example, fire safety and prevention, caring for our planet, the indispensability of trees). Children create pages and are asked to describe the significance of these visualizations as they relate to their own, or potential experience. Again, their words are written as they are dictated, and by the end of the year most are able to pick out words that they recognize.

Art: another tool for learning

It is incumbent to nurture an awareness of the beauty and diversity in our world. Addressing the arts illustrates in a non-threatening manner that we are all different in so many ways. Furthermore, children learn to appreciate music, beautiful art, and nature as instrumental in finding peace within themselves.[8] Their calming influence helps lead to greater open-mindedness and acceptance of individuality. Children learn that:

- Some people like the red or blue or black crayon, but others favor the green or yellow or purple.
- Some people like rock and roll music, and others prefer classical.
- Some people like the flowers in the garden, while others would rather look at the insects and critters.
- Some people like onions…while others don't even like chocolate![9]

Art is the use of creativity, skill, and imagination to create something that's beautiful or emotionally expressive. Our approach to art is unique in that children partner with an adult for a particular project. By guiding them individually in the process, children are more able to focus on what they are doing rather than being distracted by what the others are doing. They learn decision-making, personal preference, foresight and vision, as they plan how different materials can be used to create objects that add beauty to their world.

---

[8] *One three year old was admitted into the program after being expelled from two preschool programs. After several weeks I was able to see why this had occurred, in the class disruption alone. But you can't kick a little kid out of preschool three times before he is even four years old! He went on to attend GP for a second year. As we celebrated our 10th anniversary when he was 11, he and his Mom came to our Open House. They had come to thank me for getting him on track through nurturing his interests in art and nature. He was wearing the icon over-sized GP t-shirt he had made when he was four.*

[9] *One child told us, "My favorite thing to eat is food, chocolate food." "Eeew, gross!"*

A strong art program nurtures creativity while it fosters learning. Creating art enhances self-control, fine motor skills, visual perception, and the ability to interpret the environment, while encouraging reflection and self-expression. Art increases a child's level of confidence through personal accomplishment. It teaches kids that skills vary between individuals; and to support one another in their endeavors. They discover that they have control over the finished product, that everyone's choices are unique, and that what matters is being satisfied with their own work.

Children love to make art. By sharing their completed artwork, they experience reinforcement for their endeavors, and learn to appreciate the efforts and individuality of others. A strong introduction to the arts at a young age goes a long way in developing solid underpinnings for the lifelong expression of creativity.[10]

Music: an integral part of our day

Growing Places Kids are introduced to the world of music through song, rhythm experiences, movement, and exposure to the many types of music.[11] This offers further initiation to the diversity in our world. In our classroom, we do not limit music to a specific time; it is spontaneous and interrelated to other activities during the school day.

Music involves the whole child and can contribute to learning in many ways. It develops listening skills and auditory awareness, and contributes to speech and language development. Music involves both large and small motor skills, and can teach basic concepts, such as colors, numbers, animal sounds, etc. It gives children opportunities for social interaction and cooperation, and encourages creative expression. Music offers a release for feelings and frustrations, and adds so much joy and pleasure to our days.

Process Learning

Through the year, many of our projects are ongoing. It is important for the children to know that most "things" in their lives have a source, a backstory, and can involve a lot of effort to achieve something that is easily taken for granted. We want the children to realize there is more than meets the eye; there is a process involving ingredients, people working behind the scenes, and time.

---

[10] *See Parent Newsletter:* http://growingplaceswithkids.blogspot.com/p/expressivearts-beneficial-toeducation.html

[11] *There are lots of musicians that are geared toward children–not all of them very good. There is no need to limit kids to "children's music." Having many different types (classical, folk, jazz, new age, ethnic, country...) available broadens our taste in music, without forcing us to listen to something obnoxious over and over.*

- Much of our food comes from farms. We will go to an orchard to pick apples, watch them pressed into cider, and make applesauce and dried apples. We might make peanut butter and jelly sandwiches from scratch (grind the peanuts, make the jam or jelly, bake a loaf of bread).
- Making Stone Soup is an annual event. Not only is it an expression of sharing, the kids' involvement in making it compels them to try, and even like things they would not have eaten otherwise.
- Ice cream is quite different from the ingredients we start with. As are the beads we make from clay, poke holes in, bake, and then string.
- We like to visit construction sites in the neighborhood and see the progress being made; or watch a tree that is being taken down and talk about the ramifications of its removal.
- We create books that illustrate the many facets of who we are, and the world in which we live.
- We will work for days making Christmas art and Valentines; and delight in the joy of delivering them to people the children don't even know at the Senior Center.

We want the children to look deeply into their world, appreciate the details, and the roles they have in making the world a better place.

> *"Making a garden is peaceful. Trees grow in the garden and fruit grows in the trees. When I eat the fruit I'm not hungry anymore. Being hungry is not peaceful because it doesn't feel very good. You eat and when you eat with friends that is peaceful because you use manners like please and thank you."* - Ashlyn, age 3

Social responsibility and global awareness

In this day and age, it is critical to think globally and to help our kids grow up with an awareness and appreciation of the world outside of our sheltered community. [v] Given that many of us have grown up in a small town with little ethnic diversity, we must go to greater lengths to expose our children to the gorgeous patchwork of ethnicity that makes up our world. [vi]

While some people welcome diversity in the people they associate with, others are hesitant due to various preconceptions or not understanding a different culture. Prejudice and discrimination against a certain group of people is most often the result of fear and misunderstanding. Whether a child grows up to be tolerant, or to judge people merely because they are of a certain race, religion or nationality, is largely dependent upon what is being modeled at home. Involving families in our activities through out the year is educational for them as well.[12]

We are committed to modeling social responsibility and teaching our participants the value of "giving back" to society. Given the opportunity, children discover that each and every one of us is granted powerful and unique aptitudes and blessings, no matter our circumstances in life. Children develop a sense of acceptance, altruism, and duty through various activities involving the community and broader world. They can acknowledge that while they may not share the same experience as someone else, their personal gifts can compliment those of the people around them to create a better community, and world.[13]

We live in an increasingly diverse society; the gorgeous potpourri of custom, tradition, and way of life enrich our culture. Success in today's world depends on being able to understand, appreciate, and work with others. The person who learns to be open to differences will have more opportunities in education, business, and many other aspects of life.

---

[12] *Annually, we hold a Simple Meal potluck consisting of the types of simple foods people in many parts of the world are limited to (soup, beans, rice, fruit, flatbread). Why? As adults, we know that people around the world live different types of lives. They eat different foods, live in different types of housing, speak different languages. But have you ever thought about what life is like without all the conveniences we enjoy? What if you had to carry all the water you use in a day from a river to your home? What would it be like to make meals if you had no refrigerator, freezer, or canned food? What is it like to wash all your laundry by hand? How would you function without electricity? When we share a simple meal, we have an opportunity to be thankful for the modern conveniences we have and to remember that most people in the world do not have access to such resources. We can think of ways to make our lives simpler, to unclutter our time and our living spaces. Most importantly, we can be together. We can enjoy each others company and remember that people all over the world, for generations, have gathered to share meals together. (Suzanne Blackburn)*
[13] *See parent newsletter http://growingplaceswithkids.blogspot.com/p/children-of-world.html*

Growing Places' Sister School

For a number of years *Growing Places* had a sister school in Dominica, West Indies. The children and families enjoyed corresponding with a special friend or two in another part of the world- a place where the only seasons are rain and dry, where the children and families are so impoverished that often a family of 8-12 lives in a one or two room shack with no plumbing or electricity. The children walk miles up and down mountain roads to their school, often subsisting on one meager meal a day.

Through various service organizations such as Christian Children's Fund and the Peace Corp, conditions have improved for many of the inhabitants of this tiny country (the island is 16x29 miles as the crow flies, but steep mountain terrain increases the area dramatically). There, land is rich in rain forest, bananas, pineapple, cacao, warm ocean, and sunshine.

This is very different from the experience of children in Dansville, NY and surrounding communities. Several times during the school year, the children of *Growing Places* shared artwork and letters with the children of Crayfish River Preschool in the Carib Territory of Dominica (not to be confused with the Dominican Republic).

In addition to correspondence and friendship between the children, families had the opportunity to purchase books and supplies (paper, scissors, glue, blocks...) in the name of their family or friends. Materials that we consider very basic to the operation of our classrooms changed the world of the preschool classroom in Dominica. And as the children wrote one another of their daily lives, they not only discovered the differences in each other and their ways of life, celebrations and holidays, but the very similarities in what they love, how they play, what they think about... As the families at *Growing Places* sent materials and supplies to enhance the classroom setting, the Dominican parents sent gifts of dolls and toys that are their livelihood, hand made by them for sale in their tourist trade. Eventually we were able to address the issue of malnutrition through our fundraising efforts, initiating a lunch program in that preschool. It was an amazing, educational adventure for all involved, as the children had the palpable experience of truly making a difference in the world.

After several years, we lost our contact with Dominica when the agency we worked through merged with another. We have been heart-broken to lose touch with our "sister school." Sadly, we have not succeeded in reconnecting, nor connecting with another program. The relationship between preschools required great commitment and effort on behalf of everyone involved; toil that is needed to fulfill more basic needs of these impoverished areas.

Teaching Environmental Awareness

Through a variety of field trips and classroom activities, children become aware of their natural surroundings. Children are astute in their observations,[vii] and have something to offer to the lesson as well. Once while we were waiting for the fifth chrysalis in a terrarium to open, the following conversation ensued.

Elijah asked, *"Why do we have to let them go?"*

"Because there isn't enough space in this tank for them to fly around."

"But there is lots of room in there."

"Not really, because when a butterfly flies from here to there, it doesn't fly in a straight line. They loop all around like this..."

"That's only when they're laughing!"

The more connected with nature that kids are, the more observant they become; and the more they think about how their actions affect the natural world.

> *"I don't throw my garbage on the ground. Garbage is ugly and it's not good for the animals because it will make them sick. Animals need trees and clean water and a clean safe place to live. Garbage makes the Earth not safe for animals."* William, age 4
>
> *"We have a beautiful garden at Growing Places. It's a nice place to play and animals come to live there. Fish live in the pond. We have to keep the pond clean and take out the leaves so the fish can swim and breathe. Birds live in the garden too. We feed the birds and they eat the bugs. If we kill the bugs the birds won't have enough food."* - Christian, age 3

In our garden there is a pair of cardinals, numerous chickadees, flocks of finches and sparrows, a blue jay or two, four or five squirrels, a mother rabbit, and a large toad. The little hole between the tree and brick path is a chipmunk's burrow. The closer you look, the more you will see: the spider web next to the pond, the aphids sucking the life out of the honeysuckle, and the ladybugs munching on the aphids!

The birds have particular perching spots that they return to time and again: the fence post, the bush next to the parking lot, the wisteria, the tree at the back of the property... They seek food, squabble amongst themselves, and cooperate! We watched two sparrows collecting nesting material while a third kept watch for danger from the telephone wire; after a time, the sentinel flew down to assist in gathering while one of the others took a turn at sentry.

Different types of birds have different calls for different situations. We usually hear a bird before we see it, and learning to recognize its song before we locate the bird is good practice for learning to read (distinguishing between similar sounds helps to prepare a child in learning to discern between consonants when it comes to phonics).

Children who are afraid of bugs overcome their anxiety by studying insect behavior:

watching a bee gather pollen; a spider weave her web; a colony of ants collect bits of cracker dropped near the hedge. Likewise, children who go to a window or the porch during a thunderstorm to watch the clouds, lightning, and rain, locating the direction of the storm, calculating the distance, are usually not afraid of thunder.

We count the different kinds of plants, birds, and insects in the garden (*"Look! A laughing butterfly!"*). We lay in the grass and look up into a tree, watch the clouds. Creating an intimacy with the natural world makes it impossible not to think about how the way we live affects this planet and all of life. The teachable moments become innumerable as we see a blue jay pecking at a cigarette butt, a cat eating a bird, a plastic bag blowing against the fence. Asking children questions will help them give their logic and reasoning centers a workout (e.g., *"what would happen if an animal got stuck in that bag?"*) We start giving thought to the weed killer we consider putting on the lawn, or the bug spray we are tempted to use on those horrible aphids.

"But if that poisons the bugs, won't it poison the other animals?"

"If we kill all the bugs, what will the birds and toads eat?"

"If we waste paper, they will have to cut more trees down. Where will the birds and the squirrels and the bugs live"

Growing Places Kids participate in caring for their planet by conserving, reusing and recycling on a day to day basis.

- Families start to participate in *Earth Hour*[14] and *Earth Day*[15] activities through the year as they are more exposed, through their children, to the impact they personally have on the environment.[16]
- We use reusable dishes, cups, silverware, and shopping bags.
- We incorporate our compost into the garden.
- We have moved away from use of toxic fertilizers, weed killers, pesticides, or cleaners; and mix our own earth friendly concoctions on premises.
- We make paper from scraps in the classroom; and reuse household items in art.
- We use a Have-a-Heart Trap in the event of mice, and remove the insects and spiders that invade our indoor space to the outdoors.

For the sake of our planet, ourselves, and the future of our children, it is critical that we take action every day, in reducing the amount of harm that we unintentionally inflict on our Mother Earth. We all know this.

A thorough make-over of our way of living is a daunting task if we don't tend to keep environmental awareness at the forefront of our daily round. Of course things get busy;

---

[14] *Earth Hour is an annual global lights-off event uniting people to protect the planet. See* https://www.earthhour.org/

[15] *Earth Day is on April 22. It provides an excellent opportunity for each of us to take inventory of our personal impact on the environment; and to make certain adjustments, alter our current lifestyle to minimize the negative wallop we each have on the environment.*

[16] *See parent newsletter:* http://growingplaceswithkids.blogspot.com/p/a-few-simple-ways-that-you-can-teach.html

we have too much on our minds to give it much thought as we whirl through our day to day lives. There are varying degrees of intentional living. Making more of an effort to be deliberate in choice and action, and raising our children to do the same, might seem intimidating. But if we approach this in baby steps, a week at a time, diminishing wasteful behavior becomes more manageable.[17]

We feel that it is important to plant the seeds of environmental awareness and responsibility at an early age. If this notion is established and nurtured at a young age, children are more likely to be sensitive to the wonder and fragility of the natural world, and develop a commitment to protecting it as they grow older.

Getting Parents on board as we begin...

Families are encouraged to visit *Growing Places* before the school year begins. Assisting in the preparation of the classroom gives a child a sense of ownership and belonging, easing the transition into a new environment. During this visit, we acknowledge the child's (and parent's) ambivalence as they embark on this journey. Having feelings validated lessens the pain and instills confidence.

- *"It's a little bit scary when you go someplace new and don't really know anyone. I always feel shy on the first day too."*
- *"It's really hard to let go when your child has not been beyond the circle of love and protection you have created."*

It is easier for some children to be desensitized to separation anxiety through a gradual lengthening of the school day during the first week. On the first day, we tell little ones that the parent will be back in one hour for snack and story. *"That's how long Sesame Street is on."*[18] If they would like to bring their favorite doll or stuffed animal to keep them company, they may. [19]

We explain to children and parents when they come in, that when the teacher says it's time for the parent to leave, they will leave. Even if a child is upset, it is much easier for everyone if the caregiver simply exits. Hesitation to separate just proves that there is reason to be afraid! A child's upset passes *much* more quickly if they make a clean break.[20]

---

[17] *http://goldenratiodesign.com/growingplaces/wp-content/uploads/2014/08/Earth-Day-Every-Day-2016.pdf*

[18] *Parents are encouraged to coordinate going for coffee during this time, giving them a chance to start getting to know one another, as well as to commiserate in their own separation anxiety. This is often the genesis of highly valued life-long friendships.*

[19] *Treating this comfort object as someone who is important to the child (inquiring about its name and things that they like to do together) provides an excellent opportunity to open communications with a child.*

[20] *See Parent Newsletter: http://growingplaceswithkids.blogspot.com/p/school-days.html*

In the beginning, some children are heartbroken when Mama or Daddy leaves, but quickly adjust. Others cry daily for a week or two. One little three-year-old had an extended period of distress until I gave her a medal for bravery, "*because you have come every day even though you were afraid to be away from the people you love.*" She wore that thing for almost two months because it helped her to feel more confident. One little guy was angry to tears when his mother left, yelling in his deep voice, "*open the do'!*" over and over for the first 45 minutes of that hour. He was quiet and stand-offish the second day. Once given the job of hand-washing supervisor, his confidence grew and he became a leader in that class. Shy children often remain on the sidelines and watch, sometimes for minutes, sometimes for days. I will go and hang out with them while the other kids play, before excusing myself to get back into the fray, inviting them to join when they are ready. Invariably there comes a point when they can no longer tolerate sitting on the sidelines while the others appear to be having so much fun. By the second week, while there may be some hesitation on the part of a few, most of the kids bounce into the building with nary a wave goodbye to the person who brings them.

While some kids become distraught when their parents leave, a little one who is feeling more comfortable can be encouraged to make a special effort to connect with one who is upset. Even inexperienced children are sensitive to whether one of their peers is in need of TLC or one-on-one attention by the teacher, and capable of rallying to compensate on their behalf.

The first days are spent in free play with little structure at all, allowing the children to get to know one another and their environment. Each group of children has it's own personality: where some groups thrive on make-believe, others love to make art and music, hang out with a good book, or do explorations in science. The teacher observes, mediates as necessary, and identifies child and group needs and preferences.

Reluctant children can be enticed to come back by asking them to bring a healthy snack the next time they come. If kids are bringing in snacks, fruit, nuts, veggies, cheese and whole grain crackers are good choices.

We solicit parents' help by asking them to give their kids a good breakfast before they come in the morning. Many parents do not have a good understanding of the nutritional needs of young children and may need some guidance. It's not hard to find breakfast/snack foods that can help to stabilize a child's blood sugar all morning:[21]

- Whole grain toast with peanut butter; add a piece of fresh fruit, or canned without added sugar.

---

[21] *Sweet, sugary snacks are not helpful! If a family must bring cupcakes in for a birthday treat (usually with a thick layer of frosting and sprinkles), we have snack a half hour before the children leave because it takes precisely 22.5 minutes for the sugar buzz to kick in, and it isn't pretty. Sugar affects everyone's blood sugar, some more than others. It causes a spike in the blood levels of glucose (the body's usable form of sugar), then a rapid drop. In some kids, this can show up in a burst of high energy, followed within an hour or so by sleepiness, irritability, or poor concentration. Whenever a child is exceptionally tired, cranky, whiny, or completely wild, nine times out of ten they tell me they had a sugar-laden breakfast. Source: Pam Maxson, Health Educator Nicholas H. Noyes Memorial Hospital*

- Some ready-to-eat cereals that are lower in sugar than others, like plain Cheerios. Hot cereals are good, but watch the ingredients list because almost all of the "instant" types have loads of added sugar.
- Yogurt with fruit is an excellent choice if one starts with plain yogurt. Flavored yogurt is loaded with sugar.
- A cheese or peanut butter sandwich on whole grain bread may appeal to some children in the morning.
- Foods to avoid include highly sweetened cereal, pop tarts, anything dripping with syrup, doughnuts or pastries, cookies, etc. Granola or fruit bars disguise themselves as healthy choices, but they too are laden with sugar of some form.

At the beginning of the year, it is a good idea to get a handle on food sensitivities (dairy, gluten, red dye) within the class, and to keep a stash of allergy friendly alternatives available. It has been my experience that most children are very resolute in their acceptance of the fact that they can't eat certain things.

In addition to addressing dietary needs, parents are asked to help their child in asserting his/her independence by sending them to class in clothes that can be put on without assistance, avoiding buttons and buckles wherever possible. It is helpful to everyone to send a child out into the day with pull-up, elastic wasted pants and Velcro shoes, as it is not always convenient to interrupt what we are doing to buckle overalls or put together complicated outfits. Children must be taught with patience, as many times as it takes, how to use buckles, buttons, snaps, and such. Three and four-year-olds are old enough to learn these things. It's also beneficial to have extra clothes on hand in the event of an "accident."

It takes time and effort to connect with parents on a level that allows us to work in tandem in grounding a child. It is so important to get on the same page as far as what is expected of a child, so that s/he has a consistent frame of reference for developing self-discipline.

Family involvement is pivotal

Participation in special events and activities by parents, siblings and grandparents is encouraged throughout the year.[viii] One of the things that makes this program unique is opposite of the "trickle-down effect." Parents and families get a taste of the learning that is occurring in their children and tend to support that learning by modifying their own actions.

Furthermore, making parent involvement a requirement allows families to become an integral part of a child's participation in the program. [22] Day to day operations, grounds keeping, and repairs are a way to draw other family members into the *GP* community. Children have the opportunity to have a look at what goes on behind the scenes as well. Setting aside time for a work party two or three times a year provides a clear opportunity to satisfy these responsibilities, as well as to provide community-building within the organization. Many of the endless but necessary tasks have been accomplished in this way.

Tasks for Parent Helpers

Fall Clean-up	Inside Jobs	Spring Clean-up
Rake leaves and brush out to curb	Kitchen Fairy	Paint and weed planters
Mow, weed and whack	Clean carpet, wash floor	Remove dead shrub
Level ground (fill dips and holes)	Cover/organize books	Trim/fertilize shrubs
Clean out shed	Holiday Decorations	Till garden
Repair Fence	Replace ceiling lights	Stabilize rocks around the pond and get pump running
prepare for	Wall paper, paint	Weed around pond
Pumpkin Contest	Install tiles	Mow, weed and whack
Harvest Festival	Minor repairs	Take stuff to the dump
Winter Solstice	Book keeping	Hang art displays around town and take them down
Plow	Copy/collate newsletters	

There are also many opportunities for people who stay at home with children, or work outside the home during the day to become involved:

- Typing letters and articles for newsletters
- Doing computer work: book keeping, website development, social media updates
- Baking for special events
- Preparing project materials for the teacher
- Telephoning to pass along information or solicit help
- Making fliers and posters
- Organizing events: taking the lead on the Pumpkin Contest, for instance

---

[22] *Disclaimer: Parent helpers on a typical day tend to be disruptive to the child and the group. I have found that it is easier to be the only adult in the room, unless there are extenuating circumstances: a special project, event, or a child with special needs. This is one of the advantages of keeping class size small (six children is ideal) That's not to say that back-up is not arranged in case of an emergency. When the children are signed in, there is a phone number given for each adult responsible for that child during class time. Arrangements are made for one of the caregivers to be readily available (within the building, or nearby) in the event that assistance is needed.*

- Public relations: hanging fliers, preparing presentations, attending festivals on weekends
- Mailings: updating contact list, collating newsletters or fundraising materials

Children need ongoing reinforcement and modeling of these behaviors as they proceed through their lives to become the best person they can be. It is important to get on the same page as far as what is expected of a child, so that s/he has a consistent frame of reference for developing communication skills, self-discipline, social and environmental responsibility.

CHAPTER
FOUR

Establishing the
Roots of Peace

> *"Peace is quiet and playing with quiet toys. You need to share. That means giving the toy to someone else sometimes. Taking a toy away from someone is not peaceful. If someone has a toy you say, 'please can I have that?' And you wait for your turn. You say, 'please can I have a turn on the rocking chair' if someone else is using it."* -Nolan, age 4

Teaching self-discipline and effective communication are tantamount in grounding a child in Peace. Children need to be nurtured with encouragement, love and security; and instilled with a capacity for self-discipline. They more readily thrive when given a solid foundation of experience in behavioral expectations and consequences, and the tools to express themselves effectively.

　　Discipline is often thought of in terms of punishment, which more often than not teaches a child to be angry and fearful, and that power is what counts. Alternatively, it can be characterized as a rule or set of rules governing conduct, involving self-control, will power, and consequence. It provides clarity, stability, and intention.

Kids need guidance in terms of defining what behaviors are unacceptable (e.g., being disrespectful, hurting others, stealing, lying, breaking things), and providing suitable consequences for misbehavior. Self-discipline enhances impulse control, making appropriate behavior more likely.

Children need and want to be given guidelines, to know what to expect, and to feel safe. When creating boundaries for young toddlers and preschoolers, we remind them that the bottom line is safety. Little kids can make sense of this; being afraid or in danger is not peaceful.

Kids who are given clear limits regarding the expectation of non-violent play and appropriate behavior develop a deeper understanding by letting them think about the reasons for the boundaries that are set. They become more able to see how their behavior impacts others, and vice versa.

- Biting, hitting, kicking, pinching, pushing and throwing things at people hurt. It's never okay to hurt someone; and it's never okay for someone to hurt you.
- It's not safe to be wild in the classroom because there just isn't enough room- you might get hurt or break something.
- We have to keep things picked up so no one trips on them and gets hurt.

Children need boundaries to develop a strong sense of self. In setting limits, consequences that are relative and proportional to misbehavior should make sense to a child. This works to provide clarity in decision making as well. For instance:

- If you're not careful with your library books, the librarian won't let *you* borrow more.
- If you are mean to your friends, they won't want to be *your* friends anymore.
- We can go outside today only if *everyone* is going to be a good listener so we can *all* be safe
- Temper tantrums are never the way to get what you want. *You* need to calm down, talk it over, and work it out with words.
- *You* will lose privileges if *your* responsibilities have not been fulfilled;
- If you destroy that in anger, *you* will have to use your allowance to replace it; and make amends for damaging something that doesn't belong to you.
- If you take something without permission, *you* are the one who must return it.[23]

Before giving an ultimatum, we must ask ourselves whether we plan to carry out this action, or if this is an empty threat- one that there is no intention of following through with. This type of threat is a desperate attempt to regain control over a situation, and children will challenge us to see who is actually in control.

If we give a warning that we intend to follow through with, we need to make sure that it is an appropriate consequence to the misbehavior, and that it is fair to everyone involved. We want to avoid punishing other class members for one child's misbehavior.

---

[23] *Having the children in conflict draw a beautiful picture for one another provides an excellent do-over, helping them both to feel better and to become better friends.*

The fearful child

Instilling fear as a means for discipline is not helpful. For example, receiving a shot is a fear common among children. I have heard a parent telling a child that if she doesn't behave, the doctor is going to give her a shot. Needless to say, this child is terrified and becomes frantic when she has to go to the doctor.

Needles are scary to many of us. The trick is to be honest and matter of fact about the object of fear, sharing with a child, "I don't like getting shots either because they hurt, but only for a minute. They don't hurt as much as when you stub your toe, or bite your tongue, or bonk your nose. I wish you didn't have to get a shot too, but shots are so people don't get very bad sickness, and to help people get better..."

As parents and teachers, we are given the responsibility of teaching our children to be confident, capable and productive citizens. We must create a safe environment without instilling unnecessary fear, by communicating caution in a rational way. It is difficult to live a confident existence if one is afraid to take the next step toward a desired achievement.

This task can be challenging given that we live in a fearful world. We need to keep our children safe from danger while tempering our own fears. Children are extremely sensitive to the emotional response of the people around them, and will respond in kind: they become fearful in varying degrees, ranging from healthy caution to paralyzing fear, largely based on cues received from those around them. For instance:

- It is good to be cautious of strangers, but one must be careful not to exaggerate the sense of danger where it is unwarranted. Approaching the topic of stranger danger can be done in a matter of fact way: "Some people are bad; but most people are good. It is okay to say hi when a stranger says hello, but never go with someone you don't know unless mommy or daddy tells you that it's okay..." I was in a public restroom and a woman in the stall next to me said to her child: "You stay right with me. If you don't, someone is going to steal you and you will never see mommy or daddy again. Do you want that to happen?!" A child who is fearful of all strangers becomes immobilized in the face of new situations involving other people.

- I happen to be afraid of open heights. Being the mother of four rambunctious children, I did not want them to suffer the incapacitation of my fear. Kids can be fool-hardy creatures, climbing the highest tree, or jumping off of a cliff into the river. I had to force myself to watch them graduate from one level of difficulty to the next without excessive interference, at times against my better judgment. Thankfully they were able to grow into the confident, skilled climbers that they are today. They are able to experience a whole world which remains inaccessible to me, as I remain rooted in fear at the foot of a mountain while they scamper up mighty peaks.

Time Out is a useful tool that we all need occasionally. Usually, all that is needed when things start spiraling out of control is to be removed from a situation. A small chair, or a bottom step located within sight but set aside from the focus of activity, is most useful in beginning to teach little children self-discipline. For young children, a minute or two is long enough (a simple rule of thumb is one minute per year of age). It may be necessary in the beginning to calmly, gently, and matter of factly hold a little one down in the seat. Time out provides an opportunity to distance the child (or oneself) from a volatile situation, and to settle down. Time out is also helpful when something is being required of a child (picking up toys, getting ready to go somewhere): You can offer the opportunity for them to do the job, or to sit in Time Out, and *then* do the job. When kids are clear about what is expected of them and why, time out is rarely necessary.[24]

On the other hand, some children are a lot more challenging than others. It's not that they are "bad" kids. They (usually) are not intentionally misbehaving. When working with an extremely active and impulsive child years ago, I was beginning to feel at my wit's end. I came to dread the days that he would be in attendance. Together, we created a behavior and accomplishments checklist for us to go over together at the end of the day. It helped him to become more aware of his actions and to keep them on track. He came to an event four or five years later and it was such a joy catching up with this engaged and endearing fifth grader. He told me that he learned to listen at Growing Places, and *"that's when I learned to be peaceful."*

Classroom Behavior and Accomplishments[25]

Name	Date	Date	Date	Date	Date	Date	Date	Date	Date
Is Polite									
Listens									
Settles Down									
Uses Reading Manners									
Shares- uses words									
Stops When Told									
Stays Safe									

Parents and teachers need to be consistent, and on the same page regarding discipline; otherwise children gain the upper hand by playing one off of the other. A child with clear limits knows where they stand. Expectations are made clear, and appropriate disciplinary

---

[24] *Most useful in getting a child to do what needs to be done is to make a game of it. Challenging the kids to do what is required before you count to 20 is an effective ploy for getting them to comply. "See if you can pick up those toys before I count to 25; go get your shoes before I count to 10..." It almost always works. Singing the Clean-up Song is effective as well: "Clean up, clean up, everybody everywhere. Clean up, clean up, everybody do your share"-by Frank Olsen, for Barney*

[25] *The Me and My World books that the children work on through the year, and their art portfolios serve as our only means of "progress report."; with the exception of the above Classroom Behavior and Accomplishments checklist, which can serve as an instrument for self-assessment when needed.*

measures are followed through with as necessary. If children expect a certain outcome each time they misbehave in this manner, they learn that it is not okay to act this way; and if they do, there are consequences.

There are many ways to communicate

We tend to forget that there are many ways to communicate. What child does not understand a nod or shake of the head, a beckoning finger, an index finger to lips, a scowl, or a sincere look of approval?

A child who is acting out is communicating that certain needs aren't being met: they may be hungry or tired or upset about something, or just need a hug. Paying close attention to what children have to say, and how they are behaving, is what is needed.

Children need to be taught specific language necessary for expressing their feelings and resolving conflicts peacefully. Given the opportunity, little kids become quite good at working things out between themselves. If we take a child (particularly an only child) and put them into a group of kids, we can't expect that child to be able to get along with the others just because we tell them to. We have to model how to work out disagreements, and "spoon feed" the specific words to use.

- "Tell him- *'I don't like it when you do that, it's annoying, please stop.'*"
- "Say-*'I don't like it when you laugh at me. It makes me feel bad.'*"
- "Say- *'I'm using this right now, you can use it when I'm finished with it.'*"
- "Tell her-*'I don't like when you grab things away from me. You have to wait for your turn.'*"
- "Say- *'It makes people feel bad when you say mean things. Please stop.'*"

Likewise, we learn about negotiating, and coming to an agreement through discussion. Again, we must give them the specific language to use.

- *"You can go first this time, but I get to go first the next time."*
- *"Let's play my game first, and then we can play your game."*
- *"How about if you use this toy for now, and we can trade in five minutes."*
- *"I really love blue. Please can I use it first and you use a different color? Then we can trade."*

It never ceases to amaze me how quickly children respond to each other once they learn to communicate in this way. This is reinforced during circle time by discussing how to respond when faced with a difficult situation.

> *"Sometimes friends hurt each others feelings. Sometimes they might hit you or make you bump your head. When my feelings are hurt I say, 'I don't like you- you're not my friend anymore.' I wanted to make her feel bad but now I feel bad. Now I feel grumpy. That is not peace..."*
> Dawsyn, age 4
>
> *"Being angry does not feel peaceful. Hurting someone when you're angry is not peaceful. If I'm angry I can jump up and down. Roaring like a lion when I'm angry is peaceful. Closing my eyes and falling asleep is peaceful."*- Erin, age 3

By having these conversations at a time when they are not in the throes of emotional reaction to a situation, children are usually able to stop a disagreement long enough to think through what we have talked about. They begin to learn self-discipline.

We need to keep in mind that actions speak louder than words. Children reflect our attitudes regarding prejudice, forgiveness, the environment, our lifestyle. They grow to exhibit the values and actions learned in their home. A child whose parents use force, learns that this is how one gets what they want. Ask just about any kid who hates bugs and snakes, and invariably Mama or Daddy hates them as well. You can pretty much bet when you see a little boy struggling like the dickens not to cry, that he has been taught that "*big boys don't cry- crying is for sissies.*"

As a parent and teacher, one may start to feel like a broken record, repeating the same words of advice or reprimand over, and over, and over. If a little child is engaged in another activity, or with someone else, they have the capacity to tune out every other thing; they are not even aware that someone is speaking to them. You might begin to wonder if you should refer this child to a hearing specialist.[26]

On the other hand, so often the assumption is made that the kids aren't paying attention when we discuss things with other adults regarding our issues in parenting, financial concerns, marital difficulties, grandma's terminal illness, or current events. Believe me when I say they are listening. We need to remain vigilant to their presence when discussing matters that may be upsetting, misconstrued, or place little ones in a position of taking sides. These conversations are not meant for little ears. [27]

Young children take things literally; they are not yet able to distinguish a figure of speech from actuality. Once when I said, "*I'm pooped!*", a little guy responded, "*you better wipe yourself!*" An off the cuff remark like, "*I'll die if I don't get that job,*" will instill an incapacitating fear for your life if overheard by your preschooler.

It's when you think kids are not paying attention that they take notice. They realize

---

[26] *When my eldest was in kindergarten, he came home with the paper ear pinned to his shirt indicating that he had had his hearing tested that day, I fully expected to receive a phone call with the dreaded news that he was hearing impaired!*

[27] *When 9/11 occurred, one little person thought every time she saw the towers fall on TV, that another building was hit. She was terrified that the school her mother was attending the next evening would fall as well.*

that when you hang their artwork on the wall, you appreciate the work that went into it. They remember the times created especially for them: the effort put into a special event on their behalf; the choice of a book or favorite snack in their honor; time set aside to give them your undivided attention. They even come to understand that the reason you "yell" when they are doing something foolhardy, is because you love them and want them to stay safe.

Our days are immersed in play

As critical as play is in child development, in these times it becomes almost an after thought as a result of the prevalence of electronic devices, our hurried lifestyle, changes in family structure, and increased attention to academics and enrichment activities. Lots of play time is crucial to the development and well-being of children.

Play is a potent vehicle for establishing strong roots in self-discipline and effective communication. A majority of our time is spent in free play while each child has one-on-one time with the teacher to work on a given project. Games and puzzles, artwork and make-believe are selected to relate to our theme for the day.

During playtime, in an effort to minimize the chaos and distraction of too many choices, the group is limited to two or three sets of toys at a time (chosen together by the group during *Welcome Circle*). Before the kids get something else out, it is required that one set of playthings is put away. Everyone is expected to help pick up.

We steer away from gender specific activities such as princess and gun play. *Growing Places* is a peaceful place, and we don't even pretend to shoot and kill people. And given that many three and four-year-old girls are obsessed with princesses, parents are encouraged to leave the gowns and let that play happen at home.

While many children initially lean toward more stereotypical roles in play, boys will take on the mantle of nurse, daycare provider and wait staff as readily as girls come to wear the hats of doctor, fire fighter, and cop…. The girls play with the train tracks, vehicles and construction toys, the boys in the kitchen and taking care of the babies, without complaint when those are the play choices for the day. Thankfully, it has become much more socially acceptable for boys to participate in play involving dolls. If a little one comes to class with a cherished baby-doll or furry friend, we:

- Try to remember their names and treat them as honored members of the classroom; though if they are a distraction they can "watch" from the sidelines.
- Talk directly to the doll and assume that it has feelings. This will allow a child to recognize and express their own feelings.
- Use the doll to act out any problem situations with a child. For example, "Will you help Clara be brave when she goes to the dentist?"

Extensive play time allows opportunities to discover a capacity to be kind, and loving, and honest. A child who treats dolls or stuffed animals as friends is building social skills which help them to make real friends. They feel love and caring toward these imaginary friends. It is a chance for them to practice their sharing skills, and express their feelings. Through play, children learn how to deal with their emotions, accept one another, and begin to discover their place in the world.

They learn that each person has special gifts and distinct tastes: Some people are skilled at putting puzzles together; some are able to run really, really fast. Some are good at helping someone to feel better; some are better at finding things. And sometimes we need the help of someone who is better at doing something we have trouble with.

A clear sense of personal talents and preferences leads to greater acceptance of self and others, allowing children to reflect, recognize, and value their own individuality. Children learn that each person is different from everyone else; we are like the blossoms in a garden, each flower necessary to create the beautiful landscape in which we live.

It is so much easier to learn in an accepting, peaceful setting, where everyone knows what is expected. Children become more able to follow directions, sit quietly for story time, and participate in class discussion. They learn the importance of listening, being polite, reaching out, empathizing, accepting one another, and celebrating differences.[28]

---

[28] *This approach to peace education is shared in detail with parents so that we may come to be on the same page regarding behavioral expectations.*

FIVE

Fertilizing the Garden

Feeling isolated is common as we enter the into the unknown territory of being a parent, especially if there is no extended family nearby. When life changes dramatically (for example, a child is born, one gets sober, or relocates to a different community) it can be difficult to know how to connect with a new circle of friends. Having a gathering place for people embarking on a path that is so fraught with uncertainty, provides a sense of security in the knowledge that resources and moral support are available.

> **Growing Places Parent Center:**
>
> **('grōiNG /plāsəz̸/perənt/ 'sen(t)ər)** *: noun, verb, adj.*
> **1.** an informal gathering of parents and caregivers away from the confinement of home; **2.** an excuse for a morning out with the child(ren); **3.** a place to laugh, share, commiserate and be foolish over a cup of coffee; **4.** a place for preschoolers to make friends with other children and adults; **5.** an opportunity for toddlers to observe and have some involvement with Playschool activities through field trips and special events, making the transition easier when their time comes to move up; **6.** an invitation to the broader community to become involved; **7.** a center for the volunteer activities critical to the operation of our programs; **8.** a source of information on parenting and family issues; **9.** an opportunity to share talent, expertise and ideas in helping to make Growing Places a quality resource for our children; **10.** a must for any parent who ever longs for a change of scenery and conversation with another adult.[29]

We are given the immense responsibility of raising a child with little or no actual training. Many of us have only the example of our parents, many of whom were coping with their own struggles, or otherwise ill-equipped for the job. But how do we go about accomplishing this if we haven't been taught, or at least had a good role model?

At *The Parent Center*, parents are exposed to various means and methods for raising children through participation in our programs. A parent center provides an opportunity to meet and create community with others traveling the path through early childhood. Access to such a supportive environment as parents learn the ins and outs of raising children changes the landscape of parenting dramatically. People with more experience are there to offer a variety of solutions and model more effective ways of communicating with children. Parenting is no longer such a lonely and random endeavor.

When forming a community-based *Parent Center*, the first order of business is to gather a group of four or five enthusiastic and committed people to attend to the details of creating and running a program for parents. These folks are responsible for planning and oversight of activities.

Our *Parent Center* has been an off-shoot of the children's programs. It grew out of the playgroup created by parents back when we were first getting started. It could easily be a stand alone entity, or the seed that bears the fruit of further programming for children. It was the parents and caregivers of a playgroup that expanded *PC* offerings by developing the following resources.

- **Infant/Toddler Play Groups** have been offered for parents with children aged six months to three years. These are best limited to six children, with one of the (adult) participants taking the lead as a committed presence or host of the group. Upon

---

[29] See **http://goldenratiodesign.com/growingplaces/parent-center/**

entering into a playgroup, parents fill out a *Parent Needs Assessment*[ix] to determine format and structure of the group best suited to their needs. At times it is necessary to reconfigure a playgroup to address temperamental needs of the children. For example, an extremely rambunctious three-year-old may overwhelm a younger, mild-mannered group of children. It may be necessary to find a better fit with a different existing group of children; or provide the impetus for creating another, more active type of group.

- **A Resource Library** offers parenting books, children's media (books, movies, music), and recommendations for places of interest. A parent newsletter provides a glimpse into what's available within the *GP* community, as well as seasonal activities, advice on how to face parenting challenges, healthy kid-friendly recipes, and a calendar of community events and resources.

- **The Red Cross** sometimes has babysitter training available to teens in the area. Finding a trustworthy babysitter can be a challenge. The *Parent Center* may take on sponsorship of a group of trainees, with referral service for those who have been certified. CPR classes are another possibility.

- **Monthly Family Fun Days** are activities held throughout the year to which family members are invited. Some of the special Playschool activities and field trips are offered to playgroups and homeschooling families as well. Toddlers and younger siblings get a taste of being part of the older group.

- **Parent workshops** offer a series of informal discussions with early childhood professionals for parents during play group time. These are facilitated by a consultant (speech therapist, librarian, music teacher, school based prevention worker, and other community resources) for the purpose of answering questions and alleviating concerns.[x]

- **Support Groups** may offer general support, or address a specific issue.[xi] Decisions need to be made as to whether the group will be time limited (six weeks) or on-going. Will the group be open, or closed to newcomers?

- **Parent Education Series**: *Common Sense Parenting in a World That Doesn't Make Sense* In a world increasingly fraught with anxiety in bringing up children to be loving, responsible, and happy people, *Growing Places* offers a unique approach to parent education. The twist in this parenting course comes in being brought into your child's inner world as you rediscover your own creativity through make believe and art activities, which will be incorporated throughout discussion of the wide variety of issues facing parents today.[xii]

- **Homeschooling Co-op** offers resources, assistance in curriculum development, gathering place for group activities, and community with other home-schooling families[xiii]

The Parent Center has been a valuable resource for many young parents, and caregivers. Numerous lifelong friendships have germinated here. It offers a clearinghouse of possibility and information allowing parents to determine their own values and approach to parenting. It has been instrumental to the success of this organization as well. Through monthly group activities and service projects, support networks among parents create a venue for the strengthening of the broader community.

Tree Top Haven

Tree Top Haven is the proverbial "cabin in the woods" that we long to get away to when life becomes too hectic. It offers a sense of community among women, and opportunities for personal discovery and growth[xiv] in a nurturing environment. Women in particular, fulfill so many needs of family and community that there is a tendency to lose track of one's self and addressing one's own personal needs. It is difficult to be nurturing when there is a gaping hole in oneself that needs to be nourished.

Our heritage and life experiences influence the way we each (men and women) think and feel about ourselves, in ways that may interfere with becoming the effective parent we wish to be. Certainly, through our own upbringing, we encountered obstacles that currently interfere with our own child-rearing practices. It is within our power to shed the impact of even the most negative beliefs and experiences by integrating them in a new way.

By setting aside time for ourselves, in a very real sense we are able to give parts of our own childhood a do-over. In getting into that mind space, we are able to see things more clearly from our children's perspective. We start to become aware of the stumbles that were made in our own up-bringing, therefore making it possible to step around the same obstacles as we bring up our own children.

We have discovered that by entering a space where the expectation is the same as that for a (well behaved) three or four- year-old, we are able to shed so much of the burden of failure and disappointment that we have collected through our days and years. This is an opportunity to let go of the demands made in our day to day lives that distract us from the child within, the essence of who we are, the flame. We are reopening the world of curiosity and wonder and fun that we were blessed with as children.

In so doing we become better parents.

Making space to find ourselves

In our effort to fan the inner flame it is necessary to clear a space, remove the clutter which like wet leaves, tends to smother our soul as we go through our frenzied days. We each have a constant list running through our minds that can become so overwhelming that it all seems hopeless. Those weeds choke out the possibility of nurturing the beautiful plant that is longing to burst forth, so again, we clear the "garden bed." Clearing our minds of the nagging "have to" and "should" and "wish" and "regret" static that distracts us from the things we really want to do or think about, creates space for the achievement of inspiration and personal goals.

Creating a Master List

This is no ordinary, "manageable" to do list. This is a mind dump! A *Master List*[30] is a list of everything you think you need, or want, or wish to do or have: obligations, home improvements, events, things that you really want to do with your family, places you wish to go, shopping lists, chores, decorating ideas, recipes, every single thing that has been running around in your mind keeping you awake at night and making you feel stressed and miserable. I keep mine in a 4"x6" notebook in my purse for writing movie ideas, books I want to read, great quotes, gift ideas, garden ideas. Even if you don't use it as a check list, it serves to clear mind space so that we are able to attend to the task of self-care and personal growth. You can look back at another time and be amazed by how much you have accomplished, even if you rarely look at it. It serves as a diary of sorts.[31]

Morning Pages

Julia Cameron recommends faithful journaling in what she calls *"morning pages."*[32] Setting aside time each morning for journaling will change your life. It helps one to center; to work out conflict, anger, depression; to plan and dream... When you have those old negative "tapes" running around inside your head (*"I'm fat, ugly, stupid, a bad mother, a bitch, blah, blah, blah..."*), you can get them out, over and over if need be until they become so diluted they become meaningless; or you realize that you can only whine so much about something, and that the only way things are going to change is if you do something to change them!

---

[30] *Source: Success is a Journey: Creating a Pattern for Reaching Your Goals by Brian Tracy | Sep 25, 1999*
[31] *Remember this: So often when we are beating ourselves up for not getting this or that done, it is the result of our own unrealistic self-expectations. Once I realized that no one else knows how much I don't get done, it didn't matter as much!*
[32] *Source: The Artist's Way: A Spiritual Path to Higher Creativity Julia Cameron Mar 4, 2002*

The challenge comes in completing the three pages she feels is necessary to untangle the mess that clutters our thought processes, preventing us from fulfilling our deepest dreams and fullest potential. Now, three pages is a lot to write everyday and at times you will find yourself at a loss for what to write. So you look around you and write about the mess, or the weather, or how you want to replace that painting on the wall, or any random thing and before you know it, you have found another thread to unravel.

Writing helps to keep your mind free so that other thoughts and inspirations may enter. When you go back to reread your pages at a different time in your life, not only do you have a record of happenings, you are able to see just how far you have come on life's path.

When I get out of the discipline of writing a full three pages every day, I become out of sorts and lost. In a way this is like the *Master List*, in that it keeps your mind open to inspiration and the positive energy that helps us to create the life we are meant to have.

Overcoming the Obstacles

There are two great obstacles to taking time for ourselves: our own permission, and a free moment to do so. We tell ourselves, *"There is way too much to be done and the world won't survive without me for two or three hours. And even if it could, how could I possibly make that happen? There are the kids, and errands, and housework, and dental appointments, and the sick dog…"*

It makes sense to take some time out to rejuvenate our own spirits. How can we have the impact we desire if every bit of all that is good in us gets lost in the process of living day to day? As parents, we so often feel that we are not deserving of the luxury of self-care.

Letting go

My first conscious experience of letting go was when I was in college needing to get to a final exam on the other campus, and the shuttle bus was running late. I was fervently praying for the bus to appear, *willing* the traffic to make way for us, the lights to be green. Then it occurred to me that I would be late and there was absolutely nothing I could do about it.

Things like this happen every day as we scurry through our lives. We're in a hurry at the grocery store and get stuck behind an elderly gentleman shuffling along at a snail's pace and there's no getting past him. You're feeling desperate to get your youngest potty trained and she absolutely refuses. You need to make a connection and the first leg of your flight is delayed. A hurricane threatens your wedding day. Your car breaks down. Your teenagers are making bad choices and your job becomes to let them learn their lessons the hard way if need be. You're involved in a relationship that is not progressing in the direction you were hoping for. You're awaiting the results of a medical procedure. You can't get your spouse to stop drinking. Someone you must have contact with on a daily basis can't stand you for no apparent reason. The world seems to be falling apart and there is nothing you can do about it.

Taking a break to nurture one's soul requires being able to *let go*. Even if you are able to do that, assistance is required.

It is not easy to ask for, or accept the gift of help. Someone offers to help us do something we would not otherwise be able to do, like take a break, and we feel beholden to them to return the favor. It is not necessary or expected in most cases. People are good; they want to help. Doing something for someone in need feels good! And there will certainly be an opportunity to lend a hand to someone else down the line.

We need more random acts of kindness in this world. If we are on the receiving end, we need to learn grace in acceptance, and remember the pleasure we derive from an opportunity to do the same. Having a community of people in the same boat, allows us to give each other the possibility of taking that break that is so desperately needed.

Reconnecting to our child self: How does one begin?

When I think about *Little Ruthie*, just me playing in my room by myself, I envision the toys I loved to play with, and the naps I had to take. Nap time is not well appreciated by many children; and toys are not given the credence they deserve by adults. Yet they provide a bridge of sorts, connecting the two versions of our self.

Part of the reason I love working with children is that I get to go buy the toys I had or would have loved as a child, and then enjoy the vicarious thrill of watching the children play. Indeed, purchasing a small stash of toys to be kept in a desk drawer for times when we ourselves are feeling particularly stressed out, uninspired, or just plain needy, allows us to acknowledge the younger version of our self that to this day remains within each of us. [33] Choose your toys carefully, and collect only those that you just love. Bubbles, magic wand, slinky, kaleidoscope, Jacob's ladder, Koosh ball, Prismacolor colored pencils (expensive, but luxurious) and lovely coloring books grace my drawer. A snugly stuffed animal sits nearby to comfort me when I am sad or scared or lonely.

When my children were young, my sole purpose in the mornings was to wear them out so they would all go down for a nice long nap. But they outgrew naps and I remained cranky and lethargic until the end of the day.

When my children were adolescents, I was blessed with the gift of being surrogate mother to a one-year-old boy. In my effort to make his time in strange surroundings

---

[33] **Source:** *The Artist's Way: A Spiritual Path to Higher Creativity by Julia Cameron (Mar 4, 2002)*

with people he did not know less traumatic, I stayed in the room with him as he went down for nap, so that he would not awaken completely adrift, not knowing where he was. Little did I (nor does he) know that he gave me one of the greatest gifts I have ever received.

Nap time[34] offers an opportunity to let go of the mayhem. Not to be confused with sleeping, a nap is a chance to drift for a moment from the turmoil, to experience your inner being, your soul, the essence of who you are… That state of half sleep allows you to work out creative solutions to any number of things. Having gotten into the routine of letting my self be quiet, I realized how critical to the contentment of my soul this disconnect time has become. When I am finished, I can get up and do another full day's work.

Creativity Lost (or is it just misplaced?)

Too many times when I mention to parents the possibility of dabbling with paper and pencil, paints, or scissors and glue, the response is, *"I don't have a creative bone in my body- I can't draw a straight line!"*

There is a time in our lives when suddenly self-consciousness squelches the radiance of who we are meant to be. (One of our missions is to teach children not to let this happen) We become so concerned with what other people are thinking about us that we come to fear the full expression of who we are because someone might laugh or disapprove of something we do- if not in reality, certainly in our minds. So we hold ourselves back, disqualifying our thoughts and creations before someone else can. In reality it doesn't matter what anyone else thinks.

What matters is the sense of peace, the sense of connection with something much greater than our selves (or the greatness of our self!) when one is able to let go of outside distraction and focus on the creative and playful spirit that is within each of us.

One never truly loses the creativity that each and every one of us has been blessed with. It just becomes so deeply buried within our inhibitions that it needs a bit of coaxing.

Tree Top Haven provides not only an oasis for those seeking a break from the craziness of our lives, but a chance to reconnect with our own inner child. It is a fine place for re-discovering our creative gifts. It is a haven where one is allowed to leave the fear, heave a sigh of relief, and find our own personal niche. By taking the time to nurture our soul, we are providing a service to others: we can be a better partner, mother, employee, and person.

---

[34] *Source: Simple Abundance by Sarah Ban Breathnach (April 1,1996-)*

Getting Started

As with the other programs previously mentioned, it is desirable to have a working group, or *Steering Committee* to lead and coordinate this particular effort to

- Gather resources[xv]
- Survey the community[xvi]
- Create a plan for programming and advertising[xvii]
- Coordinate registration and confirm guest speakers

CHAPTER

SIX

Laying the Groundwork for a Program Like This

A life dream is a long-held vision of something you hope and yearn to accomplish. It starts as a niggling thought or idea, grows to become a vague wish, an intensifying desire. The vision becomes more clear and a plan starts to form, inserting itself into our thoughts, growing, taking root. It seems every waking hour becomes consumed with details of what it would look like, how it could happen. It keeps you awake at night, until there is no getting away from it, and you are compelled to take a leap of faith.

Brainstorming: Creating the Dream

Gathering a few trusted friends together for a "brainstorming session" is *fun* and doesn't cost a thing. What is needed? Who do you know that you can pull in? How can you make the most of community resources? Where will the money come from? What type of location would be ideal? Who might be compatible partners in this undertaking.

There is nothing at stake, anything goes: you can take your thoughts wherever they lead. Worksheets in the Appendix will provide a guide [xviii] [xix] [xx]

In order for a business to truly succeed, one must create a budget and then find the means necessary to finance it. [xxi] Strategic Alliances[xxii] are people and organizations that you can collaborate with on fundraising endeavors, public relations, projects, special events, and resources, etc. They stand to benefit from the coalition as well. In identifying these folks, one also gets a sense of what is already being offered in the community so that duplication of services can be avoided.

Initiating a plan of action involves creating an exhaustive list of potential advisers, role models, sponsors, and community resources, etc.[xxiii] [xxiv] These are people, places and organizations that can play a role in developing a business strategy.

In order for a project of this nature to be successful, it is necessary to assemble a strong nucleus of people who desire to be at the heart of this life altering adventure, people who can help bring the idea to fruition. Things will run much more smoothly if you are able to engage individuals who are knowledgeable in the fields of education, state law, and business/accounting, in addition to childcare providers, parents, and members of the community at large. Their creativity, skills, and devotion to children and women are tantamount to its success.

The resulting confab provides knowledge and skills in the areas you may be personally lacking, as well as connections to many of the resources necessary to get the job done. Once gathered, you have your Advisory Board[xxv], a designation which has the connotation of a more consensual and egalitarian oversight than "Board of Directors" does. A total of eight or ten board members is optimal.[xxvi]

Strong Executive, Finance, and Marketing and Public Relations Committees[xxvii] are critical to the level of success a program is able to achieve. These determine the strength of the organization as a whole, and need to be well established to move forward.

Ad hoc committees[xxviii] are formed for specific goals and projects, and may include board members, parents, and community members with expertise in a particular endeavor. Each Committee designates a Chairperson to take the lead.[xxix]

Recruitment of Volunteers

We learned the hard way[35] that it is best to accrue a roster of willing and knowledgeable helpers that far exceeds the number we think we need as we begin. Given that we rely so heavily on free labor, a carefully executed plan for the recruitment of volunteers[36] makes a huge difference.

---

[35] *As we began, volunteers were recruited as needed, starting with family, friends, and friends of friends. More often than not, we were caught short-handed. More was expected than was realistic for any one of us, and turn-over was rather high. My four children were ages 5-9 when GP was established in our home, and were enthusiastic participants from the get-go. Those kids and my husband have been my most stalwart assistants through the years. They dug gravel from our new garden space, planted shrubs, assisted with summer classes, ran errands, and posted hundreds of fliers around town. They performed at special events, painted walls, kept the ledger, and cared for the gardens. Above all else, the thing that fills my heart to bursting is the great sense of satisfaction my children took in being such an integral part of Growing Places' success.*

[36] *These resources also serve as a basis for public relations and fundraising opportunity.*

- Retired teachers often have an association or lunch bunch; and are frequently looking for a way to fill the gaping void left by the absence of young children in their lives.
- Festivals and special events are held throughout the year in most communities, offering a venue for community outreach.
- Middle school and high school guidance offices assist in placing students who have a community service requirement.
- Involving senior citizens with little kids through the local senior center is a win-win for everyone.
- There may be a Garden Club in your community that you can enlist to help with a children's garden.
- Local reading groups often consist of retirees looking for more community involvement.
- Scouts are frequently available to provide volunteer child care during meetings and special events. This serves as a venue for parents to see potential sitters in action, and kids to get their name and a recommendation out into the community.[xxx]
- Parent Volunteers: *GP* Scholarship recipients have been required to put in a minimum of service hours. Receiving a *Growing Places* Scholarship has come with the stipulation that for each $25 received, a two hour work exchange is expected during that quarter. The possibility also exists for families to volunteer and receive a $25 rebate the following quarter.[37]

One of the drawbacks of being largely dependent on volunteers, is the tendency to feel that it's easier to just do things yourself. It starts to feel like a burden to impose on someone every time you turn around. Having to explain everything over and over, and interrupt what you are doing to explain some more is time consuming and can get frustrating.

An informal volunteer orientation. including a clarification of expectations, during the welcome family potluck, or shortly after the year begins is most helpful. Posting detailed lists of tasks and expectations needed under various circumstances (class assistant, special events, work parties) alleviates much of the distraction of repeatedly showing volunteers the ropes. [xxxi xxxii xxxiii]

Money Matters

We all get tired of fund raising events. Given the current economic climate, we have found it necessary to seek extra funding beyond the usual tuitions for the coming year.

---

[37] *People who make an investment of money and time are more likely to commit more fully to the program, whereas those who receive a full tuition grant sometimes feel they have nothing to lose if a child attends only sporadically. This is not helpful to the child nor the class.*

Fundraisers have been a necessary evil to the continued operation of *Growing Places*, though we all cringe at the thought.

We have picked our means of fund raising very carefully both to reflect our mission, and to offer those who support us with unique opportunities. Great enthusiasm is a must for the success of any money making endeavor. Enlisting help from the Advisory Board is a start, but creating an ad hoc team for each fundraiser, involving parents and community members, goes a long way toward the success of the fundraiser. [xxxiv] [xxxv]

Grants are a way to receive significant amounts of "free" money that does not need to be paid back. However, so much available grant money slips through the cracks, unless you have an administrator or the strong commitment of a grant applications team. Staying on top of what's available and required, and meeting deadlines is very time consuming.[xxxvi]

It is important to keep in mind that volunteerism often becomes an "annual" in the garden of life. No matter how committed a volunteer may be, people must move along with the evolution of their own lives. A child moves on to public school; some other obligation usurps the freedom to commit to something as originally intended. A volunteer grant writer may face more pressing concerns before the fulfillment of all that is required in an application for funding. For this reason, we have not been in a position to take full advantage of the many grant opportunities available to a child/parent/women oriented endeavor focused on the arts, peace education, social and environmental responsibility.

Marketing and Public Relations

Advertising is expensive, and it is a good idea to make an exhaustive list of available venues for publicity, including relevant information (cost, deadlines, audience).[xxxvii] By identifying your target population, it is easier to decide which venues will be most productive use of your advertising dollar.

Parents of preschool-aged children are the primary target population. Stay at home Moms/Dads often choose this option because they are not ready to enroll a child in traditional preschool, or they may be educating their children at home. Because this is often a single income family, they may be more limited in funds and require scholarship assistance. Others want a small-town lifestyle, but get frustrated by lack of alternatives available to children. Working Moms are grateful to find a place that will render the loving care they are not able to provide while they are tending to their occupation.

Expectant parents are another target population. Not only do we want to plant the seed for future enrollment, they may have older children.

Daycare providers provide a link to working parents. Listings are available through the Child Care Council, which also has information regarding special activities and training.

Home educators are often looking for ways to get their children involved with other kids. Many communities have groups for home-schooling families. These can often be found through the local library, on various message boards, and in the classifieds. While listings are available through school districts, confidentiality prevents them from sharing names. It may be possible, however, to do a mailing through the superintendent's office.

Senior Citizens are an excellent resource, and may be contacted through the local senior center, office for the aging, retired teacher's association, and various reading groups. Not only will you have access to an amazing pool of volunteers; partnering young children with Seniors is fantastic on so many levels; and many grandparents have feelers out for activities for their grandchildren.

Growing Places has been an exercise in community building. The more outreach that is accomplished, the greater our success in changing the world through children.

For years we muddled through without the consistent help of a good business and finance person. In order to be successful in the long run, it is necessary to find someone to fully attend to:

- Fiscal management and record-keeping[38]
- Oversight of fundraisers
- Coordinating the processing of grant applications, including all required inspections and documentation for licensing or registration
- Marketing and Public Relations

I am a teacher, not a business person. Given that I owned the property and my husband's career allowed me to forgo a paycheck, we neglected to develop a budget sufficient to grow our financial base beyond what was needed for day to day expenditures. Given that we did not have the financial resources to hire an administrator, volunteers pieced together our financial structure. We didn't have the necessary and ongoing expertise to create an organization that could grow beyond the limited resources at hand. It worked year to year, but we really needed someone who could replace the gravel of this garden bed more fully with the enrichment that could have allowed the roots to grow deep. Upon my retirement, there was no one in the position to step in and subsidize this endeavor in the way that my husband and I were able to.

If we'd had a "how to" manual, we could have accomplished in five years that which took twenty years to achieve, and *Growing Places* would not have found it necessary to go into "hibernation."

A resurgence of this model of early childhood education is inevitable. It is our hope that these pages have created the inspiration for one such as yourself to bring it forward.

---

[38] . *Quickbooks has excellent software for non-profit organizations. In order to make full and efficient use of it, it is highly recommended to complete the tutorials or take a class.*

There needs to be a solid plan. This will involve ingenuity, and luck, and lots of input from people who are knowledgeable, and creative, and engaged. A thorough review needs to be done to determine the potential viability of this undertaking: Are you able to secure the financial means, expertise, on-going moral support and people power necessary for success? Once this is completed, there will be an easily accessible compendium of information to draw upon as you proceed.

What we lacked in financial resources and business acumen, we more than made up for in human resources, heart, and determination. Collectively, we harbored the resolve to shift a tiny piece of our world into a less competitive, more accepting and nurturing environment; where each person is able to meet their best potential and has a stake in helping others to do the same. The ripple effect of our activities has a real impact in our world through personal growth, social awareness, community action, world service, and environmental activism.

Appendix

ii. Winter Solstice: I can make the world a better place

This is the time of year that the days start getting longer- there is more light and less darkness. We each have a light that makes someone else's world brighter, and there are people and things that make our world brighter. The world is a better place because you are in it. Tell me why.

I made the world a better place because I was born. I'm a dancer and dancing is happy because I do it with my friends. Dancers make the world a better place.- Colleen, age 4

Mommy and Daddy and you love me a lot. Love makes the world better. I'm a good finder because I find stuff when you lose it. - Alex, age 3

I'm a good sister because I share my toys. When we play nicely it makes my Mommy and Daddy so happy. - Hayden, age 3

I make the world a better place because when I cough I cover my mouth so everybody doesn't get sick. I dance when I'm happy and when I'm happy it makes other people happy. - Josie, age 3

I help with the laundry and if you don't do laundry you get stinky. It's better to smell nice. - Zoe, age 4

I stay with Grandma and she loves that because we love to talk to each other. - William, age 4

I help take care of my baby sister when she's crying. I play with her so she's happy again. That helps my Mom. - Violet, age 3

I'm good at playing with my friends and when we help each other help pick up nobody has to pick up the toys all by myself. - Brynn, age 4

I play with my Gamma and go places with her and make her very very happy. When I'm a monster and a lion everyone runs and running is good exercise. - Jane, age 3

I make the world better by painting and helping my Mom cook by putting a little bit of stuff in what she's cooking so she can put in the rest. If you make food the people aren't hungry anymore. - Maaria, age 3

I make the world a better place for my boyfriend because he loves me. I'm a good friend and everybody wants to have a good friend. I help kids make hard puzzles if they can't finish. I give people good hugs when they are sad. I just be me!- Ellie, age 3

iii. Goals and Objectives

> *Our Goal is to:*
> - Enrich curiosity and flame a love of learning
> - Help children (and parents) to discover and share their gifts and talents, while helping others to recognize theirs
> - Truly embrace the differences in each other
> - Gain an appreciation for the diversity of our world, our environment, and the basic goodness of people
>
> *Objectives*
> - Through "Me and My World"[39] children will increase knowledge of self, family, and role in the community
> - Through exposure to various aspects of the community via field trips to businesses, social service agencies, cultural events, etc., children will
>   - enhance impulse control and behave appropriately in a public setting
>   - exhibit a respect for and comfort with other adults involved with their education
>   - become sensitive to the needs of, opportunities, and personal impact within the community
> - Through play and a variety of structured activities children will
>   - enhance social skills in a small group setting
>   - work and play cooperatively with other children
>   - have the confidence to participate in group activities
>   - be able to follow directions
>   - be able to sit quietly for story time and participate in class discussion
> - Through the use of various puzzles, games, and activities, children will be exposed to concepts (letters, numbers, colors, shapes) and skills necessary for a smooth transition into Kindergarten. They will
>   - have a familiarity with these concepts
>   - be proficient in the use of pencils, crayons, scissors, etc.
>   - develop a love for books and learning
> - Through involvement in our children's activities, and opportunities for personal growth, parents will begin to view themselves and the task of parenting from a different perspective, as they encourage children along life's path.

---

[39] *"Me and My World" is an on-going project involving awareness of self, emphasizing personal preferences, feelings, role and traditions within family, and place within the community.*

iv. About Friends

I have lots of friends at Growing Places. I used to feel shy and sad because I didn't know anybody but now the kids are all my friends and I love to go to school now. I know they are my friends because I am glad to see them and they are glad to see me because we have so much fun together. We love to play and build things, and make puzzles, and play hide and seek, and play play play a lot. If there is a problem we figure it out but we don't hit and grab because Growing Places is a peaceful place.- Camden, age 4

Sometimes friends give friends flowers from in the garden. Friends come to our house and you say Hi to them. Sometimes friends get mad but we say sorry and are friends again. I like to talk and play and make things and go places and eat together with my friends. My sister is my friend because I like to do that stuff with her too.- Seth, age 4

My brother is my friend. The kids at my school are my friends. My teacher is my friend and my teacher loves me. My stuffed cat is my friend because we like to play together. My dog Ana is my friend because she licks me and plays with me and goes for walks with me and I help take care of her and that's what friends do.- Silvia, age 4

My friends go to school with me. We play, and make projects, and say "good job", and decide what to play with. Sometimes I get angry with my friends but you should never hit your friends but use your words and say"I'm mad. Please don't do that anymore." - Bryce, age 4

I like Bryce because I like to play with him. I like smart kids but I don't like mean kids. I'm a good friend because I share, and play nicely, and help people, and take turns. If someone is sad, I try to make them feel better. I laugh with my friends and sometimes we go wild! -Christian, age 4

Hannah and Gage are my friends because I sometimes go to their house. Friends share toys in their room. I eat snack with my friends at school. I like to get the juice but I take turns with the other kids so everyone can have a turn. You have to wait for your turn to paint so there isn't a big huge mess. Making a mess is not peaceful but helping clean it up is very peaceful.- Carter, age 4

Friends listen to each other. It's not nice if you don't answer when someone is talking to you, but if they say mean things just ignore them. If someone hurts your feelings say "that hurts my feelings please don't say that again." Try not to hurt people's feelings because it makes them feel bad and that is not peaceful.- Kera, age 4

If you are nice to your friends they will be nice to you. If you are not nice you have to say sorry because you made somebody feel bad. I'm a good friend because I be nice and I help them fix their tower. –Samara, age 3

Being a good friend is not hitting, and being nice to each other. If my friend is sad I try to cheer them up. I try to share but sometimes they don't want to and I say "can I use that when you're done?" because grabbing is not peaceful but sharing is. Sharing is taking turns. - Mya, age 4

Elliana and Tess are my friends. I know they are my friends because they love me and we like to do things together. We play and they come to my house and I share my toys with them and we eat noodles together.- Giuliana, age 3

I am a good friend because I be nice to people. Mommy is teaching me to be a good friend. I help people when they are sad or they need help picking up the toys. Sometimes I make things for them or ask them to go to my house. -Paxton, age 4

People make friends with other people they know. Sometimes if you be nice to the person you are with, you make friends. Sometimes you just start playing with kids you don't know and they become your friends. Friends can be any age. If people do mean things you don't want to be friends. A big girl is hard to make friends with if they do mean things with your big sister. Sometimes people do mean things even to their friends and then you have to be really sorry so they will be your friend still. - Kodah, age 5

v. Service Projects

Throughout the years, *Growing Places* has been involved with a number of service projects. Please join us in helping to change the world through children by becoming involved!

Trick-or-Treat for UNICEF. During October kids across the United States collect money in the Trick-or-Treat for UNICEF box to support UNICEF. UNICEF works for the survival, protection, and development of children in 157 countries and territories around the world, helps develop community-based programs to promote health and immunization programs, basic education, nutrition, safe water supply and sanitation services, and continues to provide emergency relief as needed. Visit https://www.unicefusa.org/supporters/volunteers/fundraisers for more information.

Heifer Project International is a nonprofit organization committed to providing families and communities in developing countries with a means to earn a living. By providing a family with some type of livestock, or means for a crop, the Heifer Project teaches the people how to cultivate food for their family, and their community.. They learn to care for the animals and how to use them to generate income. A goat provides milk and offspring for sale, bees provide honey, ducks produce eggs and offspring. A family who receives livestock through the Heifer Project must contribute back to the community by giving some offspring to another family in the community. You can learn more about the Heifer Project at www.heiferproject.org.

American Friends Service Committee (AFSC) sponsors a program whereby Emergency Hygiene Kits are assembled and distributed. These kits are needed in crisis situations where electricity is unavailable and basic first aid supplies are scarce. They are distributed to refugee camps and to individual families in areas stricken by natural disaster, war, or other humanitarian emergencies. To learn more, see https://www.afsc.org/

vi. Enhancing Awareness of Other Cultures

There are many ways to expose children to the differences that exist among people, fostering an openness, respect and acceptance of people for who they are, while broadening our own experience.

- Listen to world music: *Putamayo* has a magnificent series of CD's that are a good introduction and are widely available. Some of them are geared specifically for children, but they are all fun to listen to and even proclaim "guaranteed to make you feel good"!
- There are countless ethnic folk tales and stories about children in different parts of the world. *Dorling-Kindersly* has several books about what it is like growing up in other countries (*Children Just Like Me: Celebrations; A Life Like Mine; A School Like Mine*); and the *Williamson Little Hand Series* has some multicultural craft and cook books.
- Foreign children's movies are available for rental on DVD, with subtitles, and dubbed in English and other languages.
- *GoogleTranslate* is an invaluable resource for teaching your children a few basic phrases (hello, good bye, please and thank you, excuse me, are you okay?) in various languages, the most common being French, Spanish, Swahili, Arabic, and Mandarin Chinese. For a more comprehensive experience, language learning software allows for home study of almost any language.
- Going to ethnic restaurants or having an event for which people prepare ethnic food is a way experience a new variety of flavors as well as unusual ways of eating.
- Keep your eyes and ears open for various exhibits and performances being held in area museums. For example, Memorial Art Gallery in Rochester has an interactive series of annual cultural celebrations, including Hispanic/Latino Heritage Month, Kwanzaa, Black History Month, and Asian Pacific American Family Day, offering international exhibits and demonstrations, family art activities, music and dance performances, and storytelling.
- Befriend someone of another culture living in your community. Arrange to share customs and stories about growing up in different countries and traditions.
- Sponsor a child through ChildFund International or Save the Children. This will provide an opportunity to develop a pen pal relationship with a child in another country.

vii. The Web of Life

Sharks like to eat dolphins and fish. Sharks are not bad because if they don't eat the dolphins there will be too many dolphins. If there are too many dolphins there won't be enough fish for them to eat. The fish will all be dead, then the dolphins will be die and then the sharks will die because they won't have any food either because they need fish and dolphins for food. - Christian, age 4

I don't like bees because they sting you and you cry. But bees are not bad. Bees collect nectar and bring it back to the hive to make honey and feed the babies. Bees get yellow powder stuck on their fuzziness. Then they fly to another flower and the powder comes off on the other flower and seeds grow and new flowers grow. - Shayli, age 4

Birds fly in the sky. We have to keep the smoke out of the sky because if there is too much smoke the birds might die because they can't breathe. We need birds because they help our garden grow and the birds eat bugs and if the birds don't eat bugs there will be too much bugs. - Seth, age 4

Spiders are good because they eat mosquitoes and flies. Flies are gross because they go on poop and dead animals. Spiders make webs to catch the bugs. Webs are sticky so the bugs and insects get stuck and the spider eats them for lunch. I saw a spider web at our tree house and it was beautiful. I like the good spiders that don't bite but I don't like the red ones. - Bryce, age 4

We need trees for the animals to live in. Bugs and insects and spiders and squirrels and birds need them to make their nests. Squirrels like to eat nuts. Nuts grow in the trees. Birds like to eat worms and the bugs that live in the tree. They like to eat fruit and fruit grows in trees. Caterpillars like to eat leaves. We need trees to build houses and grow our food because we like to eat fruit and nuts too. If you cut down all the trees there will be no trees left and the animals will die. - Camden, age 4

You find water in lakes and streams and in the sea at the beach. Water comes from the sky and from other water like streams go to the ocean. We need water to drink. Cows, pigs, chickens, cats need water. Ducks and fish and turtles and frogs and whales and octopuses, squids and lots of other animals live in the water. If you put lots of junk and gloppity glop in water everything would die, even trees. - Kodah, age 5

Owls hoot at night. They eat mice. Some cats eat mice too. Eagles eat mice. Snakes eat mice. If the animals don't eat the mice there will be too many mice and the whole ground will be covered with mice and we'll step on them. More mice would come in the kitchen and eat our food. Mice don't belong in the kitchen they belong outside. If we have no mice the owls and snakes and eagles might not have enough food. - Samara, age 4

We shouldn't throw garbage on the ground because the birds will eat it, and squirrels and foxes and dogs and cats will eat it. If the animals eat garbage they might choke or get sick or die. If all the ground gets covered with garbage the animals homes will be buried and they will die. - Carter, age 4

Frogs lay lots and lots of eggs in the water. They are made of jelly stuff that sticks together. But they don't all grow into frogs. Some fish eat frog eggs and some birds eat some of the eggs. If all the frogs come out of their eggs there would be frogs everywhere. They would fill up the pond and the fish would die because there isn't enough water. - Kera, age 4

We need flowers so they will grow in the garden. Mommies need flowers because they are beautiful and they smell good and make her happy. Flowers give the world beautiful colors. Elephants and rabbits and kangaroos and birds eat berries and seeds, and seeds come from flowers. - Paxton, age 4

Lions like to eat giraffes and zebras. Giraffes and zebras like to eat leaves on trees. If we cut all the trees down the giraffes will die and the lions will die because they didn't eat any giraffes for food. If you cut all the trees down, you won't have any more leaves for the giraffes and caterpillars. Monkeys and birds need trees for homes and coconuts. - Mya, age 4

Some houses at the lake get flooded but ours is up on a hill. There was too much water in the lake because it rained too much and the dock wood floated away because the water was too high. If there is more water in the lake the fish have more room to swim around! - Giuliana, age 3

viii. Special Events and Activities

Throughout the year we have special events and field trips to which parents and families (and playgroups) are invited. Depending on what the topics of the semester are, activities may include:

September	October	November
Welcome Family Potluck and Garden Party Peace Day Apple Farm/Cider Mill Square 1 Art Begins	Columbus Day Work and Pizza Party UNICEF collection Pumpkin Patch Pumpkin Carving and Decorating Pumpkin Glow, Pizza Party and Costume Parade Food Pantry Collection Begins	Harvest Festival and Family Potluck Holiday Service Project Begins
December	**January**	**February**
Tree Farm Make Cookies and Art for delivery around town Make Parent Gifts Winter Solstice Celebration	MLK Day Work and Pizza Party Sensory Fair Hospital and other community visits	Sensory Fair Valentines for Sr. Nutrition Center Make cookies for firefighters Valentine Extravaganza World Friendship
March	**April**	**May**
Peace Corp Week Simple Meal Early Bird Registration for Summer and Fall Earth Hour	Earth Day Activities Digital Detox Week	Mothers Day Tea Wild Life Management Area Community Art Displays
June	**July**	**August**
End of Year Picnic and Graduation Registration for Summer/Fall		

ix. Parent Center Questionnaire

Some things to think about when forming your Play Group:

What time frame works best for you?

M   T   W   Th   F   9-10:30   9:30-11   10-11:30

- Open (anyone can join at anytime)... or closed?

  _____

- Ongoing... or limited (e.g., six weeks)

  _____

- Unstructured (kids play, Moms visit); or some planned activity (song, game, simple craft...Moms take turns planning)

  _____

- Snacks- Have a stash available here? Moms take turns? Individual responsibility?

  _____

- Time split? so some Moms can have quiet time in meeting room, peruse parenting books, etc while others supervise kids

  _____

- Monthly topic for discussion? Check those you are interested in.

  _____ Childhood illness
  _____ Issues in early childhood (sleep, potty training, discipline)
  _____ Nutrition
  _____ Media
  _____ First aid/CPR
  _____ Stress/ depression
  _____ Behavior management
  _____ Anger management
  _____ ADHD/Autism
  _____ Daycare/Preschool options
  _____ Community Resources
  _____ Literacy

Would you be interested in being on the Parent Center Committee- helping to grow to make this valuable resource available to more people?

Are you interested in working to help with...

Special Events_____Resource Library_____Newsletter_____

x. Parent Workshop Resources

Topic	Speaker	Phone	Email	Date
Childhood Illness: chicken pox, roseola, 5th's disease, ear infections, Pinkeye, Vaccinations				
Issues in Early Childhood: potty training, bed wetting, nutrition, tantrums, sleep				
Anger management				
ADHD, autism				
Daycare options				
Preschool options				
First aid/ CPR-				
Stress/ Depression				
Literacy				
Parents as Teachers				
Communication				
Behavior management				
Community Resources				
Discipline				
Nutrition				
Media				

xi. Parent Support Groups

- *Peaceful Parenting*– Learning conflict resolution, setting boundaries and communicating with children in a peaceful manner
- *Grandparents Raising Grand Children* offered to those who thought they were finished with child-rearing but have had to step in for the parents for whatever reason. The world is a different place, and the challenges are different as an older person.
- *Single Moms* are often quite desperate for support. The Parent Center has offered mentoring for these young people, as well as a place to share the joys and frustrations of raising little ones.
- *Nursing Support Group*: It is shocking in this day and age that there can be so little encouragement for young mothers wanting to do the very best thing for their baby through breast feeding. Lactation specialists are widely available to work with moms who need a little extra support.
- *Empty Nesters* benefit greatly in knowing they are not alone as they pass through this painful life transition. The children have flown the coop! What next??

xii. Common Sense Parenting in a World That Doesn't Make Sense

Benefits:

- Parents will become more aware of a child's perspective as they find new ways to interact with their children through play and creativity.
- Parents will learn what to expect, and ways of dealing with issues specific to developmental stages of young children
    - **I. Introduction:**
        - Allowing children to be children
        - Entering your child's world: dealing with children becomes easier if you are able to see things from their perspective
        - Rediscover your creativity as you help to nurture your child's
        - Parents as teachers
    - **II. Behavior Management:**
        - Teaching your child to be "socially acceptable"
        - Communication: parenting styles
        - Anger management: understanding and dealing with your own anger
    - **III. Rites of Passage:**
        - Trials of potty training, temper tantrums, bedtime, giving up naps, dealing with bullies, etc.
        - Safety issues: teaching your child to be safe without undue fear, stranger danger, road safety, fire prevention, kitchen safety, etc.
    - **IV. Literacy:**
        - Setting foundations for reading success
        - Turning off the tube (and video games): the impact of living in a world of computers and other media, finding alternatives
        - The roles of music and art in literacy
    - **V. Childcare Options and Opportunities:**
        - Finding your best alternatives in childcare and preschool education (panel discussion)
        - Babysitting Basics
    - **VI. Growing as a Family:**
        - Teaching your child responsibility
        - Chores and allowance
        - The family that plays together stays together
            (See www.changingtheworldthroughchildren.com for details)

xiii. Homeschool Cooperative (developed with Suzanne Blackburn)

Why a Home School Cooperative?

- **Social interaction with other children and adults:**
  There are times when home-schooled children experience a need for interaction with other children of all ages, especially if they have no siblings. When a child is not used to being in a very large group on a regular basis, it can be intimidating for them to participate in large-group activities. A smaller group is a more comfortable fit for many home-schooled children. Many programs are public school related, so are not available to home-scholars. This program meets this need.
- **Shared ideas and expertise, discovery and experience:**
  Many home-schooling parents feel unsure about teaching art to their children, either because of a perceived lack of expertise on their part, or because it doesn't seem as pressing as some other areas of their chosen curriculum.
- **Shared educational resources: books, materials and equipment**

Home School Cooperative Steering Committee

- Create liaison with school district
- Determine interest in starting a home school community.
- Advertise
- Create mailing list
- Develop Survey of Needs and Expectations
- Determine collective approach
- Inventory and post resources
- Develop Curriculum
- Determine calendar

Home School Cooperative Planning Agenda

Creating a common vision

Approaches and philosophies

Objectives

Curriculum planning

Public Relations

What do we need to do

- Research Available Resources
  - Grants
  - Potential fieldtrips
- Administrative requirements
- Necessary Contacts

Topics for parent support

Potential Pitfalls

Time Line for Home School/Cooperative School Planning

- **November and December:** Contact local nursery schools. Ask about newsletters and intertest in homeschooling among families attending.

- **January:** Send out an ad, flyer, and/or survey based upon contacts made before the end of year

- **February:** Evaluate surveys or other responses to January's efforts

- **March & April:** Work on policy and format of school year involving interested families willing to get involved at this phase

- **May:** Press Release and/or ad in Penny Saver about Cooperative School

- **Summer:** Interested families meet to establish curriculum and firm up plan for the upcoming school year

Possible programs for home schooling families

- **Home School Playgroup:** Toys, books, games, nature garden, indoor slide, basic art supplies, service projects, and parenting library are available to participating families. Bring snacks or drinks to share.

- **Reading Group for Kids and Families:** This is a group for kids who are reading independently or as a family. Titles will be selected based on the interests and needs of the participating families. Younger kids can enjoy the toys and other materials while the eager readers select, read, or discuss their books. Bring snacks or drinks to share.

- **Field Trips (group rates) and Family Events:** to which home schooling families are invited. (See *Special Events and Activities*)

The fee for each session of the Home School Playgroup and Reading Group is $3 per family with one child or $5 per family with two or more children. Field Trips are usually free; the cost of family events varies. Become a member of *Growing Places* and save money on groups and events! Financial assistance may be available.

Home School Cooperative- Survey

Name:
Children's names and birth dates:

Address:

Phone/E-mail:
Most reliable form of communication:

Why do you feel that home schooling is best for your children and family?

How do you see a home school cooperative working for you? Our plan as we begin is to include science, language arts, and social studies as the "academic" subjects. The basics of reading and counting/arithmetic will be taught primarily at home and worked into the cooperative activities at levels suitable to each child. Is this a plan that works for you? Would you like to see other academic subjects as part of the cooperative? Please comment and describe any ideas you may have.

Amount of time per week/month you are willing/able to commit.

Best planning meeting times:

I am interested in participating in:

_____ Teaching (Please list your strengths and areas of expertise)   _____ Program Development

_____ Finance (budget/ grants/ fund raising/ scholarship)   _____ Business Administration

_____ Marketing and Public Relations   _____ Special Events

Do you know anyone else who would be interested in a home school co-op?

Signed _____ Date _____

xiv. Tree Top Haven Activities *(see www.changingtheworldthroughchildren.com)*

xvi. Survey of Interests *(see www.changingtheworldthroughchildren.com)*

xv. Art and Life Skills Resources

Name	Address	Phone	Art / Skill	Date	# attendees	Comments

xvii. Planning Women's Groups and Activities

Type of group:

Size of group:

Membership:

Name of group:

Frequency/duration of group:

Time:

Agenda:

Venues for Advertising

-
-
-
-
-
-

Expenses:

Refreshments:

Printing:

Books:

Scholarship:

Advertising:

Other:

Fees:

xviii. Goals and Objectives

Our goal is to:

Objectives

-
-
-
-
-

xix. Brainstorming

Describe the ideal location for your learning center- envision your dream

_____
_____
_____
_____
_____
_____

Possible Locations:

_____
_____
_____
_____
_____
_____

Where will the money come from? _____
_____
_____
_____
_____

Other Considerations:

Lawyer:_____

Accountant:_____

State Child and Family Services/Education (regulations):_____
_____

Insurance (Fire and Liability):_____
_____

Business Phone:_____

Email:_____

Website domain:_____

Potential Donors (including services)

_____
_____
_____
_____

Business Discounts- Discounts are often available to non-profit organizations and teachers (books, office/art supplies, toys, garden centers, etc.)

_____
_____
_____
_____

Suppliers- choose companies and supplies that are environmentally and socially responsible to reflect the philosophy. Buy locally where possible: even if it costs more it's better for the environment and elicits good wiil from the community

_____
_____
_____
_____

Other:_____
_____
_____

xx. Wish List

Needs	Cost	Means of Purchase (Grant, Donation...)	Notes
Furniture			
Book shelves			
Tables			
Folding chairs			
Children's tables			
Children's chairs			
Rocking chair			
Comfy chairs			
Office			
Desk and chair			
File cabinet			
Computer			
Printer			
Copier			
Phone			
Quickbooks			
Music Player			

Needs	Cost	Means of Purchase (Grant, Donation…)	Notes
Kitchen			
Microwave			
Pots and pans			
Dishes, cups, silverware			
Bake-ware, utensils			
Toys			Just the basics- avoid electronic, noisy, easily breakable, and too many
Supplies			
Cleaning			Use only environmentally sound products
Paper			Preferably recycled
Earth friendly materials			Avoid toxic, glitter, foam, etc

xxi. Budget

Overhead Expenses _____
Staffing Expenses

- Salaries
- Director or director/teacher:
- Teachers and assistants:
- Workers compensation:
- Retirement:
- Other fringe benefits:
- Substitutes:
- Food service personnel:
- Secretary/receptionist:
- Custodian:
- _____
- Total staffing expenses:_____

- **Income required to meet expenses**
- Total Income_____
- Annual Tuitions:
- Application/Registration Fees:
- Federal Monies:
- Grants:
- Cash Donations:
- Funds Raised:
- Volunteer Work and in-kind donations calculated as income
- _____

Actual Income

- Annual Tuitions:
- Application/Registration Fees:
- Federal Monies:
- Grants:
- Cash Donations:
- Funds Raised:
- Volunteer Work and in-kind donations calculated as income
- _____
- _____
- _____
- Total Income_____

Overhead Expenses July- December
(Our fiscal year has run July- June)

Expense	July	August	September	October	November	December	Total
Rent/Mortgage							
Gas & Electric							
Water							
Waste Disposal							
Phone							
WiFi							
Property Tax							
School Tax							
Fire Insurance							
Liability							
Insurance							
Lawyer's fees							
Repairs							
Postage							
Advertising							
Supplies							
Staffing							

Overhead Expenses January-June
(Our fiscal year has run July- June)

Expense	July	August	September	October	November	December	Total
Rent/Mortgage							
Gas & Electric							
Water							
Waste Disposal							
Phone							
WiFi							
Property Tax							
School Tax							
Fire Insurance							
Liability							
Insurance							
Lawyer's fees							
Repairs							
Postage							
Advertising							
Supplies							
Staffing							

Total January-June _____ Total July- September _____

Total July- September _____ TOTAL _____

xxii. Strategic Alliances

People and organizations that you can collaborate with or fundraising endeavors, public relations, projects, special events, and resources, etc.

Strategic Alliance	Address	Phone/Email	Contact	Notes
Preschools				
Daycare Providers				
Senior Center				
Middle School Guidance				
High School Guidance				
Co-operative Extension				
Red Cross				Babysitter Training
				CPR classes
Service projects				

xxiii. Ways and Means

(potential advisers, role models, sponsors, field trips, assistance…)

Type	Name	Phone #/ Email	Notes
Mentors			
Red Cross			
Library			
Hospital			possible grant source; tour
Pediatrician			
Child psychologist			
Grocery store			food donations for events; tour
Book store			discount
Pet store			
Garden center			
Farms			
Museums			
Playgrounds			
Parks			
Civic groups			
Computer wiz			website development; tech issues
			Great ad spot for newcomers to town!
Realtors			

xxiv. Community Resource People

Type	Name	Phone # / Email	Notes

xxv. Potential Board Members

Name	Address	Phone/Email	Occupation	Note

xxvi. Board Responsibilities

- **Personnel**
  - Makes assignments to executive director and monitors executive directors performance
  - Formal performance appraisal of executive director
  - Approve salary scales and job descriptions
  - Approve personnel policies
- **Finance**
  - Approve budgets for organization
  - Approve spending reports that are submitted on a regular basis
- **Planning**
  - Approve short- and long-range plans for the organization
  - Monitor effectiveness of programs to determine if they have met goals outlined in plans
- **Board Development**
  - Select new board members
  - Adopt procedures to see that excellent board members are selected and continue to serve
- **Public Relations**
  - Maintain awareness of all organization activities
  - Encourage participation in appropriate activities by the community
- **Advisory**
  - Advise the executive director on policy implementation as requested

* Members represent *Growing Places* on community-wide initiatives and official *Growing Places* business.

xxvii. Executive, Finance, Marketing and PR Committees

Strong *Executive, Finance*, and *Marketing and Public Relations* Committees will be critical to the level of success your program is able to achieve. These determine the strength of the organization as a whole, and need to be well established to move forward.

Executive Committee

Chairperson

- Facilitates monthly meetings
- Appoints committee chairs
- Signs checks, or delegates this duty to another individual
- Assures committees meet responsibilities

Secretary (or designee):

- Records and reports to members the minutes and activities of *Growing Places* on a regular basis
- Notifies members of monthly meetings
- Responsible for all official correspondence

Treasurer (or designee):

- Maintains and oversees the financial record of *Growing Places*
- Approves invoices, writes checks, provides recommendations for fee structure under direction of the Executive Director
- Provides financial report to members at monthly meeting

Executive Director (or designee, as appointed by the Executive Director)

- Responsible for the day to day operations of the corporation

Finance Committee

Budget

- Develop budget and budget policy
- Approve spending reports that are submitted on a regular basis

Fund raising

- Contact representatives
- Schedule events
- Advertising and promotion
- Party arrangements: refreshments, display area, seating, etc.
- Order merchandise
- Collect money
- Distribution of merchandise

Grants

- Research grant possibilities
- Develop time line for grant applications
- Coordinate processing of grant applications, including all required inspections and documentation for licensing or registration
- Negotiate with Department of Social Services, Child Protective Association and other agencies to serve low-income families
- Presentation of program activities to civic organizations

Scholarship

- Oversee Scholarship Fund, which will be made available to those in need, for admission into early childhood and other enrichment activities
- Develop an evaluation tool to determine need and distribution of funds
- Develop sliding scale fee schedule
- Review applications and distribute funds as determined appropriate
- Determine funding requirements, and keep board abreast of fundraising needs

Marketing and Public Relations

- Identify and target markets for disseminating information
- Develop, update, and maintain promotional materials using a multi-media approach
  - Print advertising
  - Radio
  - Social media
- Coordinate public awareness activities (e.g., presentations to civic groups, booths at community events)
  - Develop and maintain a slide show for use at these events
  - Meet deadlines for sponsorship of community events (e.g., theater productions, 1/4 Mile Kids Run)
  - Coordinate with other committee projects and promotions
  - Review items generated for public release

xxviii. Other Committees as Needed

Ad hoc committees are formed for specific goals and projects, and may include board members, parents, and community members with expertise in a particular endeavor.

Program Development Committee

- Consists of three (3) standing sub-committees (Parent Center, Women's Center, Special Events) and ad hoc committees as deemed necessary by the Advisory Board
- Cultivate list of community resources for utilization in various programs
- Develop calendars for adult, parent/family, and summer programs
- Contact, schedule, confirm and follow-up with guest speakers/artists

Parent Center Steering Committee

To ensure the success of this endeavor, a committed group of inspired parents and community members is indispensable in making sure things run smoothly, and to

- Create a plan
  - Gather information and available resources
  - Develop programs for parents
  - Coordinate parent support/toddler playgroup membership, schedule, activities, and collection of fees
  - Liaison with Playschool to coordinate group activities and field trips
  - Arrange for speakers
- Produce monthly newsletter based on compilation of *Parent Needs Assessments*
- Educate parents on availability of community resources
- Keep a calendar of events
- Advertise
  - Create list for personal invites
  - Post fliers at school
  - Post in Community Message Board/Calendars
- Keep Director and Advisory Board abreast of activities

Special Events Committee

- Identify, develop and coordinate an annual calendar of events to include, but not be limited to: holiday events, booths and activities, in conjunction with community events, educational presentations
- Assign a Project Coordinator to oversee project and coordinate volunteers
- Determine that project qualifies as enrichment
- Work closely with Marketing and Public Relations Committee

Long Range Planning Committee

- Set goals and objectives to reflect the ongoing mission and vision of *Growing Places*
- Identify, develop and coordinate an annual calendar of events, to include, but not be limited to
  - Community events
  - Marketing
  - Fund raising events
  - Grant deadlines
- Set benchmarks and time lines of goals and objectives

Personnel Committee

- Recruit and assess potential employees
- Develop a questionnaire taking legal guidelines into account
- Develop "tool" for use in rating prospective employees
- Conduct background (including credit) checks
- Act as liaison with [*welfare-to-work and school-to-work*] program coordinators
- Determine salary and benefits
- Conduct employee evaluation

xxix. Committee Chairperson

- Schedules, establishes agenda, and conducts meetings for the committee
- Apprises the Advisory Board of the committee activities and seeks vote of approval when necessary
- Keeps adequate records of committee activities
- Conducts follow-up checks on committee activities in order to assure completion of projects
- Insure accountability for any funds belonging to *Growing Places*, Inc.
- Acts as, or delegates the job of, liaison between committees, individuals, and community
- Ensures that proper channels are followed

xxx. Recruitment of Volunteers

	GP Contact	Contact Info	Meeting Date	Notes
Retired teachers				
Festivals and Special Events				
Middle School Guidance				
High School Guidance				
senior citizens				
Garden Club				
Local reading groups				
Scouts				

xxxi. Guidelines for Volunteers

Dependability: The volunteer is generally expected to work on a regular schedule as arranged with *Growing Places* personnel with whom you are working (this will vary). The volunteer will make every effort to be dependable, consistent and prompt. The volunteer will make a sincere attempt to follow through and make these obligations a priority. The volunteer will notify *Growing Places* if s/he is unable to meet his or her obligations, and keep us informed of the intent to end commitment.

Meeting Time: The volunteer shall meet with the person s/he is working with on a regular basis (as need dictates) to be agreed upon between *GP* personnel and volunteer.

Rules. Routines and Procedures of the classroom/program will be outlined by program personnel. The volunteer shall make every effort not to interfere with normal classroom routines.

Discipline and reward shall be done in a manner consistent with the classroom as directed by the teacher. In general, disciplining of the children will be left to the teacher.

Confidentiality: The volunteer will at all times respect the right to privacy of teachers and students. The volunteer will not discuss other children or classroom situations outside of the classroom (you would not want to hear someone talking about your child at the supermarket!)

Communication: The volunteer and *Growing Places* personnel shall discuss concerns immediately. If you are not happy with the way something is done or said, talk it out before it interferes with your working relationship. If necessary, get the volunteer coordinator or program director involved immediately to work it out.

Personal Conflict: If there is a personal disagreement with the person with whom you are working, talk with him or her about it at another time. Keep personal conflict separate from *Growing Places* activities.

Non-disclosure: Any information regarding *Growing Places* philosophy and program shall be considered official property of *Growing Places*. Such proprietary information is exclusively for use by personnel and those affiliated with *Growing Places*. The term "proprietary information" means any information developed by *Growing Places*, which may be acquired by the employee or member during the period of affiliation with *Growing Places*, relating to program, philosophy, activities, or written materials, and used in the development of a similar but separate program.

Please Remember: Volunteers should dress appropriately for the occasion and always sign the building log book each time you volunteer.

xxxii. **Parent Volunteer Sign-up** *(see www.changingtheworldthroughchildren.com)*

xxxiii. **Volunteer Sign-In/ Time Tracker** *(see www.changingtheworldthroughchildren.com)*

xxxiv. **Fundraising Ideas** *(see www.changingtheworldthroughchildren.com)*

xxxv. **Membership Drive** *(see www.changingtheworldthroughchildren.com)*

xxxvi. Grant Possibilities

What	Who	Deadline	Contact	Notes
Artist, Performance	Arts Council			
Health and Wellness	Hospital			
	United Way		https://www.unitedway.org/	
Child Abuse Prevention				Relative to Parent Center
Parent				
Education				
Early Childhood				
Literacy	Dollar General		https://www.dgliteracy.org/grant-programs/	
Garden				

xxxvii. Marketing and Public Relations

Venues for Advertising

- Medical facilities
  - _____
  - _____
  - _____
  - _____
  - OB-GYN, local birthing classes, hospital/birthing center
    - _____
    - _____

- Daycare providers (*see your local childcare council*)
  - _____
  - _____
  - _____
  - _____

- Extra-curricular activities, etc. (*dance, karate, music, etc*)
  - _____
  - _____
  - _____
  - _____
  - _____

- Home educators
  - Mailings may be permitted through school district
  - Home school groups
  - _____
  - _____

- New to neighborhood (Get info. to realtors!)
  - _____
  - _____
  - _____
  - _____

- Network with parents at library, in classroom, after school programs, extra curricular activities
- Use bulletin boards of work places, hospital, library
- Show case art in library display cases
- Ask permission to set up a table at school open house, kindergarten registration

Marketing and P.R. Resources

Mailings- Create an exhaustive mailing List (personal contacts, daycare providers, potential funding sources, home school groups)

_____   _____
_____   _____
_____   _____

Newspapers and Magazines

- Name_____
    - Editor_____
        - Address_____
        - Phone_____
    - Website_____
    - Expectations/ Terms of Agreement_____

- Name_____
    - Editor_____
        - Address_____
        - Phone_____
    - Website_____
    - Expectations/ Terms of Agreement_____

- Name_____
    - Editor_____
        - Address_____
        - Phone_____
    - Website_____
    - Expectations/ Terms of Agreement_____

Radio

Station	Contact	Paid advertising	PSA

Libraries: bulletin boards, brochures, attend special events, art displays

Library	Contact	Story Hour Time	Who

On-line Resources

	Name	Contact	Notes
Website Developer			
Community Home Page			
On-line Calendars			
Link to Pages			
Social Media			

85

Fliers and Brochures

Make an exhaustive list on a manila envelope for fliers, in order of location. Have a volunteer post all over town. This is a great community service project for middle or high school students!

- Schools; Daycare Providers
- Extra-curricular Activities (dance, gymnastics, music, etc.)
- Businesses and Store Fronts
- Libraries
- Churches
- Community Center; Senior Center
- Medical Facilities, including dental and optical
- OB-GYN; Childbirth Educators
- Hair Salons
- Grocery Stores/ Food Co-ops
- Work Places

Power Point/ Slide Presentations at Civic Groups (possible source of scholarship fund/ sponsorship)

- _____
  - Contact:_____
  - Meeting Time:_____
- _____
  - Contact:_____
  - Meeting Time:_____
- _____
  - Contact:_____
  - Meeting Time:_____
- _____
  - Contact:_____
  - Meeting Time:_____

Area Festivals and Parades

Festivals	Town	Date	Contact Person	Deadline	Fee
Parades					

Venues for Public Education

- Newspaper column
- Newsletters
- Journal Article
- Early Childhood Education Programs
- Childcare Council
- Cooperative Extension

Other Ideas:

Playbills for chorus concerts, school and community productions, events, etc.

_____

_____

_____

_____

Marketing & P.R. Calendar

Looking ahead to events through the year makes it easier to plan marketing strategy, and prepare materials for registrations, festivals, holidays, and other special events. If all goes well, within a few years you will be able to rely more on word of mouth.

January	February	March
April	May	June
July	August	September
October	November	December

Printed in the United States
By Bookmasters